American Illustration

American Illustration

1982/83

Edited by
Edward Booth-Clibborn

The first annual of American editorial, book, advertising, poster,
unpublished work, film animation and promotional art.

American Illustration, Inc.
67 Irving Place
New York, New York 10003

Book design by Robert Priest
Managing Editor: Lita Telerico

We would like to thank the Graphic Artists Guild for
their generous support.

Captions and artwork in this book have been supplied
by the entrants. While every effort has been made to
ensure accuracy, American Illustration does not, under
any circumstances, accept any responsibility for
errors or omissions.

If you are a practicing illustrator, artist, or student,
and would like to submit work to the annual competition,
write to:
American Illustration, Inc.
67 Irving Place
New York, NY 10003
(212) 460-5558

American Illustration, Inc.
Call-for-Entries © Copyright 1982

Published and distributed in the United States of America
and Canada by Harry N. Abrams, Inc., 110 East 59th Street,
New York, N.Y. 10022, U.S.A. ISBN 0-8109-1802-1

Book trade inquiries outside the United States and Canada:
European Illustration, 12 Carlton House Terrace, London
SW1Y 5AH, England. Tel.: 01-839-2464

Printed and bound in Japan by Toppan Printing Company.
Paper 128 GSM matt coated

Typefaces: Franklin Gothic Condensed
Century Schoolbook

Mechanicals: Mary Moriarty

Published by Polygon Editions S.a.r.l.,
Basel Copyright © 1982

Contents

Introduction

Ideas are funny things. They can be good, bad or indifferent. They can be easy to see—in your own mind's eye—but hard to translate into reality. Sometimes they can take a hold on your mind and fret and thrash at it like a dog might deal with an ancient slipper. At other times, an idea and its realization can be a process as smooth as drawing a glove onto your hand.

This first edition of *American Illustration* has been both dog and glove.

I've wanted to produce such a book for about five years. At the outset the idea seemed simple enough. We had had so much success with *European Illustration* it seemed all we had to do was follow the same route and another successful book would emerge. But I'd reckoned without the sheer size of America, and had dismissed the practical difficulties of working across the great Atlantic divide.

However, these difficulties were overcome and so here it is, the first edition of *American Illustration*, a book devoted to the pursuit of excellence in illustration in America.

I must say, here, how much of a debt of gratitude I owe to a small group of people who, like me, wanted to produce a book which would encompass all that's best in American illustration today, without having to include the invidious business of awards, prizes or cliques. These people— Robert Priest (Art Director of Esquire Magazine), Mary Shanahan (Freelance Art Director), Marshall Arisman (Illustrator and Co-Chairperson of Media Arts at New York's School of Visual Arts), Linda Johnson (Freelance Art Director), Steve Heller (Art Director of the New York Times Book Review), Marc Crawford (Editor-in-Chief, Time Capsule Inc.) and Julian Allen (Illustrator)—did more than simply help enormously. In fact, the existence of *American Illustration* owes a great deal to their energies, to their will to see it live and to their shared belief in the idea that a book like this has a place in the world. Indeed, it is, in many ways, their book. It reflects much of what they believe to be good in illustrative work today. With their help I was able to bring together a first-class jury whose ultimate selection (which you'll see here) is the distillation of over 5,000 items submitted by professionals and students from all over the country.

What is surprising is the way in which our jury has, in this first edition of *American Illustration*, plumped mainly for the work of traditionalists. I don't mean by this that they have selected work by imitators of the Brandywine school (although, in the work of Liz Pyle, we have images created by a distant relative of the great Howard Pyle). It's more that, in choosing work by people such as Milton Glaser, Seymour Chwast, Brad Holland and R.O. Blechman, they have created a platform for this series which has as its base what I can only call the 'establishment' of the American school of illustration.

This is, of course, no bad thing. We are determined to select only what is best in this subjectively judged field. It is also a first-class principle from which to go forward. I hope it will not deter anyone from submitting their work in the future. More importantly, I hope it will not prove a bar to those many fine illustrators whose work I would like to see given more respect and acclaim.

In part this giving of acclaim is the purpose of *American Illustration*. Yet our objectives are broader than the simple act of recognition of high standards achieved over a long working life, or even acclaim for brilliance at the beginning of a career.

Both I and the members of the Committee believe in the inherent value of good illustration and in the principle of encouragement by example. So we hope that, if you are a student of illustration, you will submit your work for the next edition and that, if you are no student but a devotee, you will find much in these pages to enjoy and admire. For our part, we see our task as being to make a positive contribution towards both the improvement of illustrative standards, and the appreciation—by the public at large and other illustrators—of the talents of those who our jury considers to be the most outstanding artists of the year.

EDWARD BOOTH-CLIBBORN

The Jury

Ronn Campisi
Chief Designer, Boston Globe, Boston

Ronn Campisi has been Design Director of the Boston Magazine, The Real Paper and Fusion Magazine. Currently he is the Chief Designer of the Boston Globe.
His duties include designing the Globe Magazine, overseeing the design of the Sunday Globe newspaper and working on special projects.
He has won well over 100 awards working with the Globe Magazine.

Henrietta Condak
Art Director, CBS Records, New York

Henrietta Condak, a graduate of Cooper Union, has worked for Esquire Magazine, McCall's Magazine, and Gentlemen's Quarterly. She has held a wide range of freelance accounts, from fashion to corporate. Currently working at CBS Records, where she became Senior Art Director of Masterworks in 1980, she is also a member of the faculty of the School of Visual Arts and has been on the jury of various publications and organizations. Her album covers have been featured in all the major graphics publications. She has won numerous awards for her work, including a gold medal from the Art Directors Club.

Louise Fili
Art Director, Pantheon Books, New York

Louise Fili has been Art Director of Pantheon Books since 1978. She is also Consulting Art Director for Writers and Readers of London and has served as Art Director for Congdon and Weed of New York. Prior to Pantheon, Ms. Fili spent several years as Senior Designer and Art Director at Herb Lubalin Associates.
In addition to her responsibilities at Pantheon, she designs book jackets and books for other major publishing houses and is an instructor at Parsons School of Design. Ms. Fili is a member of the New York Chapter of the American Institute of Graphic Arts, and her work has won acknowledgment from the Art Directors Club of New York, the Art Directors Club of Chicago, the AIGA Book Show, the AIGA Cover Show, AIGA Insides, the Type Directors Club, the Society of Illustrators, and Graphis Annual.

Rudolph Hoglund
Art Director, Time Magazine, New York

Rudy Hoglund, Art Director of Time Magazine since June 1980, has been involved in various and diverse aspects of the newspaper and magazine business. He started off working for the Newspaper Enterprises Association in the comic art department. After several years creating his own cartoons, he moved to New York City to become the Art Director of the entire organization.
He studied in New York with Milton Glaser, who in 1976 offered him the position of Art Director at More Magazine. At More, Hoglund worked closely with Glaser and Walter Bernard. In February 1977, Hoglund and Bernard began redesigning Time Magazine, and in the summer of that year Hoglund joined Time as Deputy Art Director, for which he has won several awards. In 1979 he helped redesign Adweek Magazine.

John Macfarlane
Publisher, Saturday Night Magazine, Toronto, Canada

John Macfarlane began his career in journalism as an editorial writer at Canada's national newspaper, The Globe and Mail. Before leaving newspapers for magazines, he served as Entertainment Editor of The Globe and Mail and the Toronto Star.
He was Editor of Toronto Life Magazine, Executive Editor of Maclean's Magazine and Editor of Weekend Magazine prior to joining Saturday Night as Publisher.
He is Director of Magazines Canada, the National Magazines Awards Foundation and the author of weekly television commentaries on the mass media.

Woody Pirtle
President & Creative Director, Woody Pirtle, Inc., Dallas

Woody Pirtle's multifaceted design firm offers graphic consultation and creative services to major corporations. Pirtle has been honored in local, regional, national and international design competitions, was named Communicator of the Year by the Art Directors Club of Houston in 1979, 1981, and named Communicator of the Year by the Dallas Society of Visual Communications.
Pirtle recently conducted a design seminar for Herman Miller Company employees, and was invited to join the Alliance Graphique Internationale, of Zurich. Recent exhibitions have been held at the Cooper-Hewitt Museum, the Art Directors Club of New York, the Maryland Institute of Art and the American Institute of Graphic Art in New York City.
Pirtle is also very active in educating students, judging design and advertising shows, lecturing, and participating in various workshops and seminars throughout the country.

Kerig Pope
Managing Art Director, Playboy Magazine, Chicago

Kerig Pope has been with Playboy Magazine for the past fifteen years. During this time, he has won all the major awards that are available for both his own illustration and design, as well as work he has commissioned. Prior to this, he worked as Art Director at Mercury Record Corporation, designing album covers.
Kerig was trained as a painter at the School of the Art Institute of Chicago. In 1973, along with 9 other painters, he represented the United States at Sao Paulo Bienniale. He has shown paintings at the Smithsonian Museum, the Whitney, the Art Institute of Chicago and the Museum of Contemporary Art in Chicago.

Hans Teensma
Freelance Art Director, Colorado

Born and raised in Holland, Hans Teensma began his professional work in design and photography in San Francisco as Art Director of Outside Magazine. Following an interlude at Rolling Stone in New York, he moved to Denver to launch the new Rocky Mountain Magazine. Within a span of three years, the magazine established itself as a major outlet for illustrators and photographers and was awarded numerous design and editorial honors, including the National Magazine Award for General Excellence in 1982.
Based in Colorado, Hans now works as a Consulting Art Director in the print media, a photographer and a book designer.

Illustration **Edward Sorel**

Editorial

This section includes illustrations for newspapers and their supplements, consumer, trade and technical magazines and periodicals.

Blair Drawson Artist
Louis Fishauf Designer
Louis Fishauf Art Director
Canadian Opera Company Souvenir Catalog Publication

Drawing in Canadian Opera Company Souvenir Catalog to illustrate
the opera Tales of Hoffman by Offenbach.
Watercolor.

18

Kinuko Y. Craft Artist
Skip Johnston Art Director
National Lampoon Publication
NL Communications, Inc. Publisher

Cover illustration for National Lampoon magazine's
"Sin" theme issue, February 1981.
Egg tempera on gold leaf/gesso wood panel.

19

Marvin Mattelson Artist
Joe Brooks Designer
Joe Brooks Art Director
Penthouse Publication
Penthouse International Ltd. Publisher

Illustration depicting Arab influence over American banking
for an article entitled "The Selling of America"
by Ernest Volkman in Penthouse magazine, April 1982.
Acrylic.

Marshall Arisman Artist
Frank Devino Designer
Frank Devino Art Director
Omni Magazine Publication
Omni Publications International Ltd. Publisher

Illustration for an article about the artist entitled "Where Flesh and
Steel Mesh" by Douglas Colligan in Omni Magazine,
January 1982.
Oil on canvas.

21

Michel Guiré Vaka Artist
Muney Rivers Designer
Robert Priest Art Director
Esquire Publication
Esquire Publishing, Inc. Publisher

Illustration for an article entitled "Looking for a Hovel"
by Richard Higgins in Esquire Magazine, October 1981.
Dyes and watercolor.

22

Blair Drawson Artist
Martine Gourbault Designer
Martine Gourbault Art Director
En Route Magazine Publication
Southam Printing Ltd. Publisher

Illustration for a destination piece by Niloufer Marker
in En Route Magazine, December 1981.
Watercolor.

23

Mel Odom Artist
Kerig Pope Designer
Tom Staebler Art Director
Playboy Publication
Playboy Enterprises, Inc. Publisher

Illustration for an article entitled "The Sunken Woman"
by Joyce Carol Oates in Playboy magazine, December 1981.
Watercolor.

Brad Holland Artist
Vincent Winter Designer
Vincent Winter Art Director
Inside Sports Publication
Active Markets, Inc. Publisher

Illustration for an article entitled "Something's Rotten in Foxboro" by
Steve Marantz published in Inside Sports, February 1982.
Acrylic.

Wolf Erlbruch Artist
April Silver Designer
Robert Priest Art Director
Esquire Publication
Esquire Publishing, Inc. Publisher

Illustration for an article entitled "The Limits of Tolerance"
by Page Stegner in Esquire magazine, July 1981.
Oil.

26

Dagmar Frinta Artist
Nina Scerbo Designer
Nina Scerbo Art Director
McCall's Working Mother Publication
McCall's Publishing Co. Publisher

Illustration for an article entitled "Pressures of Life"
by Carlfred B. Broderick in McCall's Working Mother magazine, April
1982.
Mixed media.

Don Ivan Punchatz Artist
Joe Brooks Art Director
Penthouse Publication
Penthouse Publications, Inc. Publisher

Illustration for an article entitled "The Gnomes of Bilderberg"
by Craig S. Karpel in Penthouse magazine, May 1981.
Acrylic.

28

Lonni Sue Johnson Artist
Nancy Rice Designer
Tina Adamek Art Director
Postgraduate Medicine Publication
McGraw-Hill, Inc. Publisher

Illustration for an article entitled "Juvenile Rheumatoid Arthritis" by
John J. Calabro, M.D. in Postgraduate Medicine,
September 1981.
Watercolor.

Thomas Woodruff Artist
April Silver Designer
Robert Priest Art Director
Esquire Publication
Esquire Publishing, Inc. Publisher

Illustration for an article entitled "Leonore"
by Roberta Smoodin in Esquire magazine, April 1982.
Watercolor.

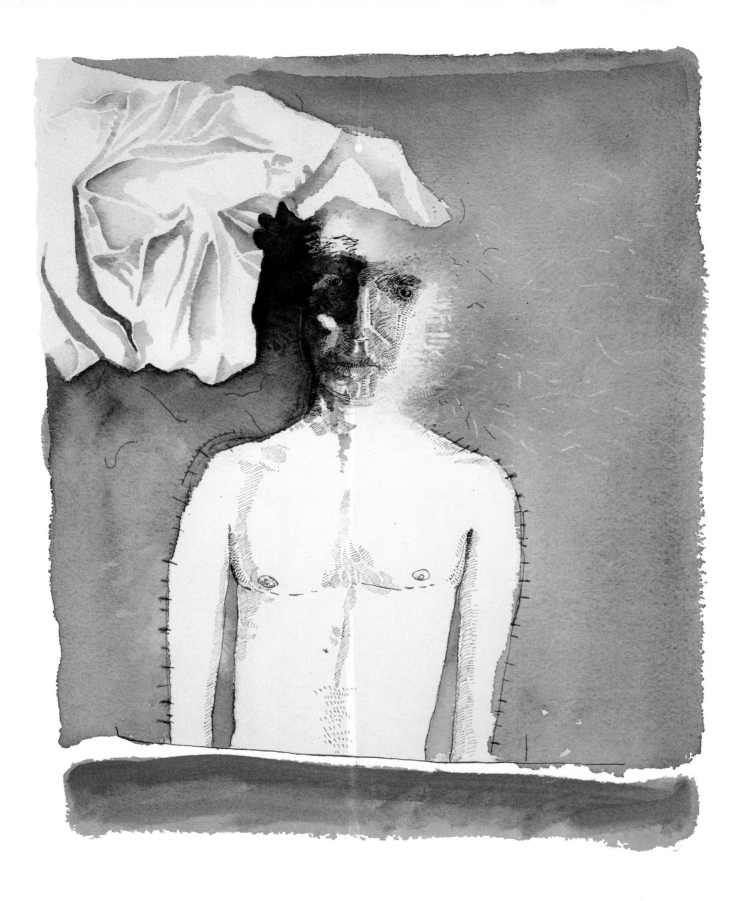

Alan E. Cober Artist
Mary Zisk Designer
Mary Zisk Art Director
Science Digest Publication
The Hearst Corporation Publisher

Illustrations for an article entitled "Cults" by Flo Conway and Jim
Siegelman published in Science Digest magazine, January 1982.
Watercolor and pen and ink.

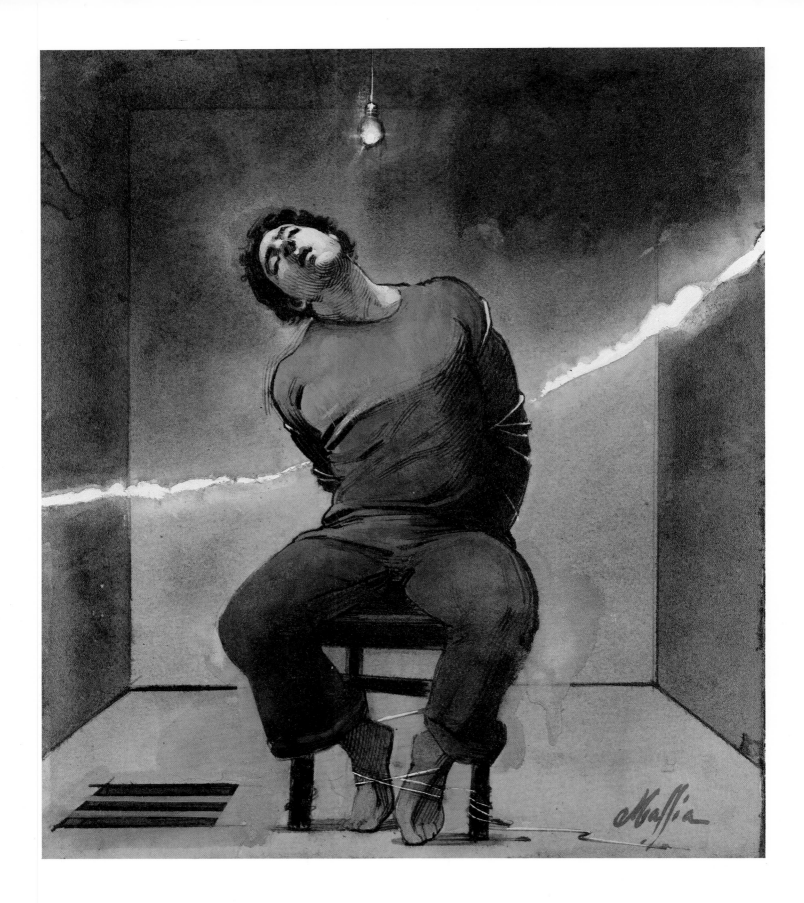

32

Daniel Maffia Artist
Greg Paul Art Director
David Beach Writer
The Plain Dealer Magazine Publication
The Plain Dealer Publishing Co. Publisher

Cover illustration for The Plain Dealer Magazine, February 8, 1981.
Mixed media.

Vivienne Flesher Artist
Ronn Campisi Designer
Ronn Campisi Art Director
The Boston Globe Magazine Publication
Globe Newspaper Co. Publisher

Illustration for "The Owl," a fiction piece by John Auerbach
in The Boston Globe Magazine, April 5, 1981.
Pastel.

34

Blair Drawson Artist
Stephen Costello Designer
Stephen Costello Art Director
Quest Publication
Comac Communications Ltd. Publisher

Illustration for an article entitled "A Matter of Life or Death"
by Nicholas Regush in Quest magazine, October 1981.
Watercolor.

Janet Woolley Artist
April Silver Designer
Robert Priest Art Director
Esquire Publication
Esquire Publishing, Inc. Publisher

Illustration for an article entitled "The Public Family" by Francisco
Goldman in Esquire magazine, June 1981.
Oil and collage.

© Barbara Nessim Feb 6. 79 BN

36

Barbara Nessim Artist
Franco Raggi Designer
Franco Raggi and Rosamaria Rinaldi Art Directors
Domus/Moda Publication

"Redhead with Lines" opening page painting for ten-page fashion
spread in Domus/Moda magazine, October 1981.
Gouache with pen and ink.

37

Renee Klein Artist
Terry Koppel Art Director
The Boston Globe Magazine Publication
Globe Newspaper Co. Publisher

B&W illustration for an article on Latin music for Calendar Section of
The Boston Globe Magazine, April 29, 1979.
Linocut.

Marshall Arisman Artist
Martha Geering Designer
Louise Kollenbaum Art Director
Mother Jones Publication
The Foundation for National Progress Publisher

Illustration for an article entitled "Teamster Madness"
by Douglas Foster in Mother Jones magazine, January 1982.
Acrylic.

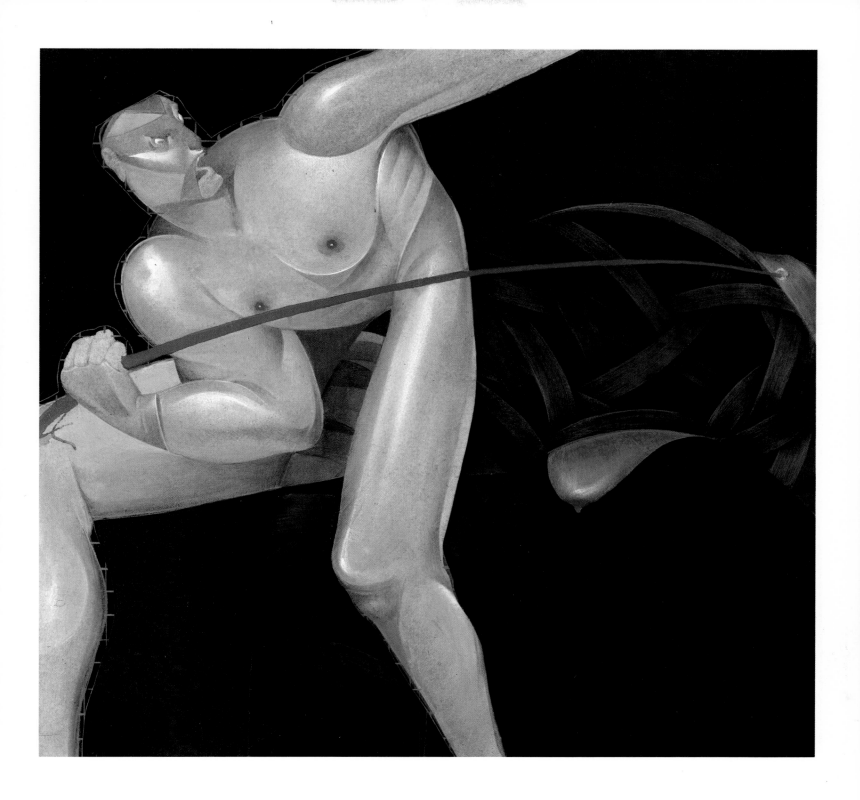

Anita Kunz Artist
Art Niemi Designer
Stephen Costello Art Director
Quest Publication
Comac Communications Ltd. Publisher

Illustration for "The Hating Game" by Maxine Sidran
published in Quest magazine, October 1981.
Acrylic.

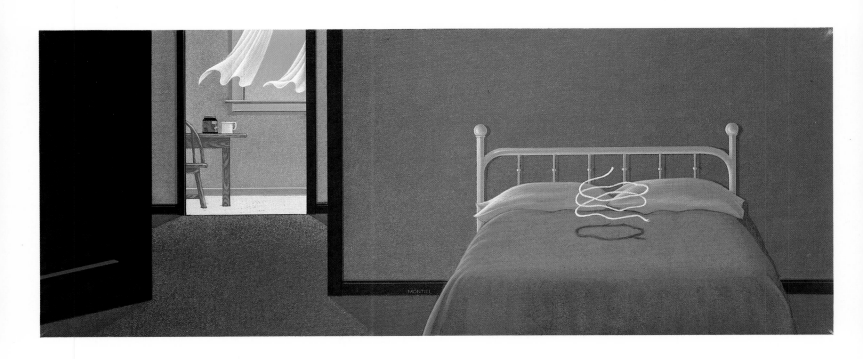

40

David Montiel Artist
Diane Lamphron Designer
Diane Lamphron Art Director
Ms Magazine Publication
Ms Magazine Corp. Publisher

Illustration for an excerpt from the book *Bodily Harm* by Margaret
Atwood in Ms Magazine, April 1982.
Acrylic.

41

Wilson McLean Artist
Claire Victor Designer
Joe Brooks Art Director
Penthouse Publication
Penthouse International Ltd. Publisher

Illustration for an article entitled "Young, Rich and Miserable"
by Ben Stein in Penthouse magazine, April 1981.
Acrylic on canvas

42, 43

Peter Knock Artist
April Silver Designer
Robert Priest Art Director
Esquire Publication
Esquire Publishing, Inc. Publisher

Illustrations for "Starting Out to Be a Famous Reporter"
by David Halberstam in Esquire magazine, November 1981.
Gouache and watercolor.

Dagmar Frinta Artist
Michael Grossman Art Director
National Lampoon Publication
NL Communications, Inc. Publisher

Feature illustration for a short story entitled "Henry Sprague, Mental
Patient and Failure" in National Lampoon magazine,
April 1982.
Watercolor and mixed media.

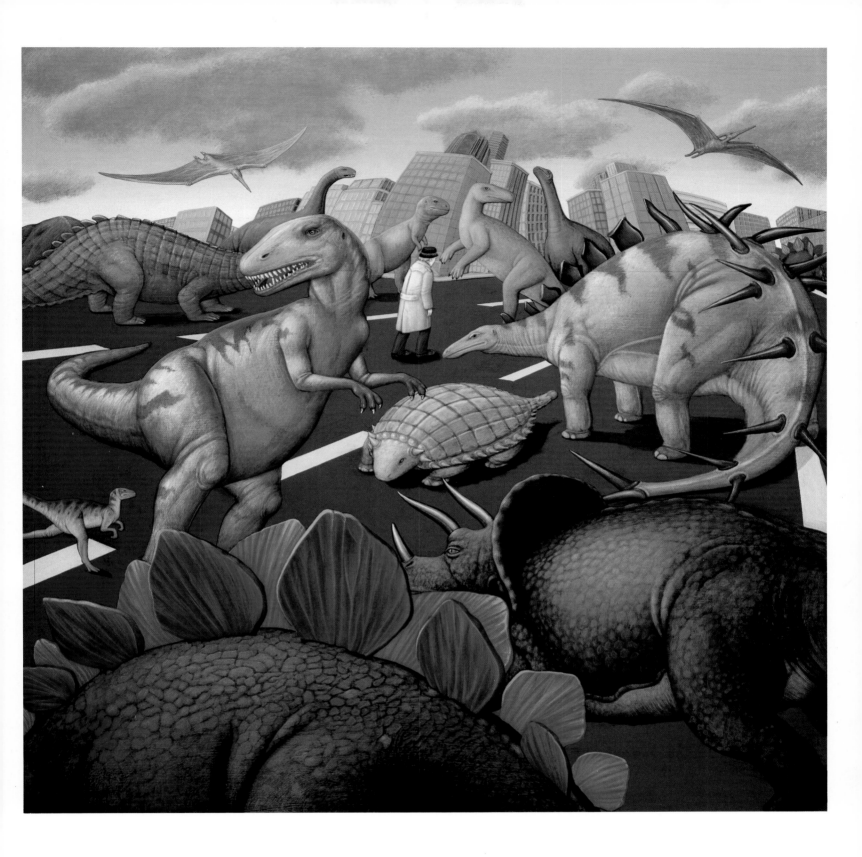

Kathy Calderwood Artist
Kerig Pope Designer
Tom Staebler Art Director
Playboy Publication
Playboy Enterprises, Inc. Publisher

Illustration for an article entitled "A Change in the Weather"
by Gardner Dozois and Jack Dann in Playboy magazine, June 1981.
Acrylic.

46

Eugene Mihaesco Artist
Nancy Rice Designer
Tina Adamek Art Director
Postgraduate Medicine Publication
McGraw-Hill, Inc. Publisher

Illustration for an article entitled "Depression"
by Mark S. Gold, M.D. and A. Carter Pottash, M.D.
in Postgraduate Medicine, June 1981.
Watercolor.

When
TV
Looks
At
Religion

Program
Listings:
Page 25

47
R.O. Blechman Artist
R.O. Blechman Designer
Susan Reinhardt Art Director
Martin E. Marty Writer
The Dial Magazine Publication
Public Broadcasting Communications, Inc. Publisher

Cover illustration for a feature article entitled "When TV Looks at
Religion" published in The Dial Magazine, December 1981.
Airbrush and brush and ink.

48

Brad Holland Artist
Bruce Hansen Designer
Tom Staebler Art Director
Playboy Publication
Playboy Enterprises, Inc. Publisher

Illustration for an article entitled
"Ruthless Mothers: Money, Values and the Gimme Decade"
by Donald Katz in Playboy magazine, September 1981.
Oil.

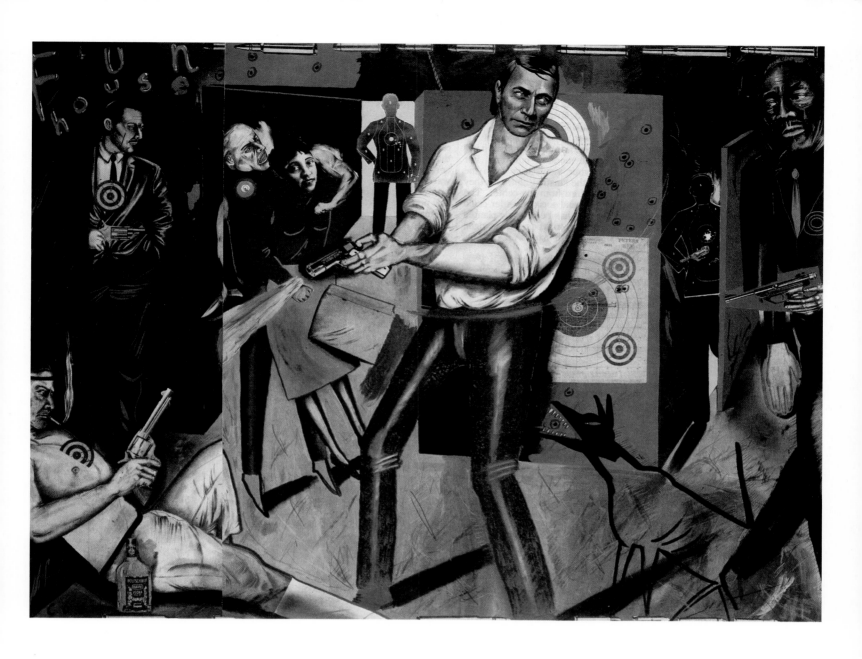

49

Sue Coe Artist
Robert Priest Designer
Robert Priest Art Director
Esquire Publication
Esquire Publishing, Inc. Publisher

Illustration for an article entitled "Shooting to Kill"
by Peter A. Lake in Esquire magazine, February 1981.
Collage and acrylic.

Julian Allen Artist

Illustration for a book entitled *Shout* by Philip Norman first used in
London Sunday Times Magazine. Subsequently printed for self-
promotion mailers in the United States, August 1981.
Watercolor and pastel.

Edward Sorel Artist
Judy Garlan Designer
Judy Garlan Art Director
The Atlantic Monthly Publication
Atlantic Monthly Co. Publisher

Illustration for an article entitled
"First Encounters: Frederic Chopin and George Sand"
by Nancy Caldwell Sorel in The Atlantic Monthly, March 1982.
Pen and ink and watercolor.

52

Cristobal Toral Artist
Claire Victor Designer
Joe Brooks Art Director
Penthouse Publication
Penthouse International Ltd. Publisher

Illustration for an article entitled "Twice Betrayed"
by Tony Angelo with Ernest Wolkman in Penthouse, October 1981.
Oil.

Liz Pyle Artist
April Silver Designer
Robert Priest Art Director
Esquire Publication
Esquire Publishing, Inc. Publisher

Illustration for an article entitled "The Death of Vigo"
by Roberta Smoodin in Esquire magazine, April 1981.
Pastels.

54

Kinuko Y. Craft Artist
Kerig Pope Designer
Tom Staebler Art Director
Playboy Publication
Playboy Enterprises, Inc. Publisher

Illustration for an article entitled "In Praise of Older Women"
by Thomas M. Disch in Playboy magazine, January 1982.
Gouache.

Kinuko Y. Craft Artist
Kerig Pope Art Director
Playboy Publication
Playboy Enterprises, Inc. Publisher

Illustration for an article entitled "My Mistress" by Laurie Colwin in
Playboy magazine, March 1982.
Oil on canvas.

56

Vivienne Flesher Artist
Susan Reinhardt Art Director
The Dial Magazine Publication
Public Broadcastings Communications, Inc. Publisher

Illustration for "Where Is Human Evolution Headed?"
by Theodore Roszak in The Dial Magazine, March 1982.
Pastels and watercolor.

Blair Drawson Artist
April Silver Designer
Robert Priest Art Director
Esquire Publication
Esquire Publishing, Inc. Publisher

Illustration for an article entitled "Going Hollywood with the Marx
Brothers" by S. J. Perelman in Esquire magazine, September 1981.
Mixed media.

58, 59

Brad Holland Artist
Kerig Pope Designer
Tom Staebler Art Director
Playboy Publication
Playboy Enterprises, Inc. Publisher

Three of a series of illustrations for an article
entitled "Rosalie's Good Eats Cafe" by Shel Silverstein
in Playboy magazine, December 1981.
Oil.

60

Sue Llewellyn Artist
Sue Llewellyn Designer
Fred Woodward Art Director
"D" Magazine Publication

Illustration for an article entitled "Stepping Out—Three Ways to
Spend a Dallas Weekend" by Amy Cunningham, Steve Kenny and
Mike Shropshire in "D" Magazine, February 1981.
Acrylic on gray pantone paper.

61

Marshall Arisman Artist
Claire Victor Designer
Joe Brooks Art Director
Penthouse Publication
Penthouse International Ltd. Publisher

Illustration for an article entitled "The Minds of Billy Milligan"
by Daniel Keyes in Penthouse magazine, January 1982.
Oil on canvas.

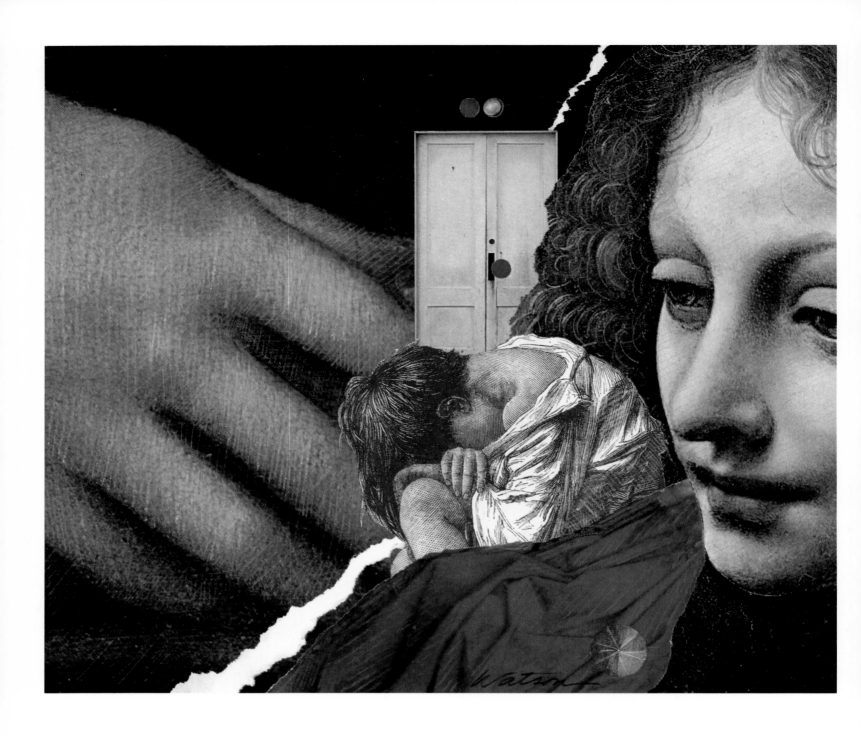

Karen Watson Artist
Ronn Campisi Designer
Ronn Campisi Art Director
The Boston Globe Magazine Publication
Globe Newspaper Co. Publisher

Illustration for a fiction piece entitled "Closed Fracture"
by Sue Miller in The Boston Globe Magazine, September 1981.
Collage.

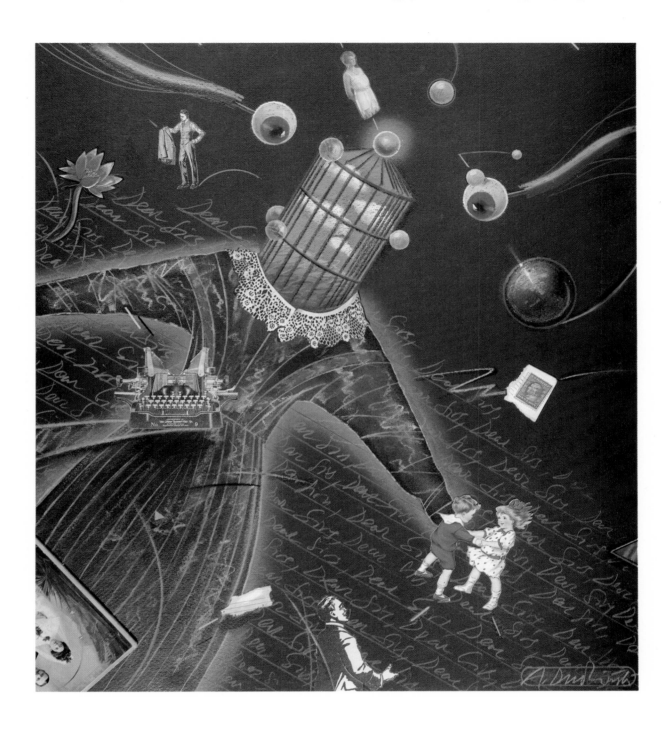

63

Andrzej Dudzinski Artist
Ronn Campisi Designer
Ronn Campisi Art Director
The Boston Globe Magazine Publication
Globe Newspaper Co. Publisher

Illustration for an article entitled "A Secret in the Family"
by Sheryl Seyfert in The Boston Globe Magazine, November 8, 1981.
Pastel and collage.

Milton Glaser Artist
Robert Post Designer
Tom Staebler Art Director
Playboy Publication
Playboy Enterprises, Inc. Publisher

Illustration for an article entitled "Death as a Way of Life"
by Christopher Dickey in Playboy magazine, October 1981.
Colored ink.

Marshall Arisman Artist
Richard Boddy Designer
Robert Priest Art Director
Esquire Publication
Esquire Publishing, Inc. Publisher

Illustration for an article entitled "White-Collar Boxers"
in Esquire magazine, June 1981.
Acrylic.

66

Vivienne Flesher Artist
Miles Abernathy Art Director
Attenzione Publication
Paulucci Publications, Inc. Publisher

Illustration for "Monster of the Greene Street Housing Project" by
Niccolo Donzella in Attenzione magazine, April 1981.
Pastels and acrylic.

67
Vivienne Flesher Artist
Gene Grief Art Director
Rolling Stone Publication
Straight Arrow, Inc. Publisher

Illustration for an article entitled "The Postman Rings Thrice for Steve
Winwood" in Rolling Stone magazine, April 1981.
Pastels and watercolor.

Jamie Hogan Artist
Ronn Campisi Designer
Ronn Campisi Art Director
The Boston Globe Magazine Publication
Globe Newspaper Co. Publisher

B&W illustration of John Reed for an article entitled
"John Reed and Other Reds" by Alan Cheuse
in The Boston Globe Magazine, February 14, 1982.
Charcoal and rubber stamp.

Julian Allen Artist
Ellen Rongstad Designer
Robert Priest Art Director
Esquire Publication
Esquire Publishing, Inc. Publisher

Illustration depicting the Reagan-Thatcher "trickle down" theory for
an article entitled "Unconventional Wisdom" by Adam Smith in
Esquire magazine, October 1981.
Charcoal pencil.

70

Janet Woolley Artist
Bruce Ramsay Designer
Derek Ungless Art Director
Saturday Night Magazine Publication
Saturday Night Publications, Inc. Publisher

Illustration for an article entitled "Summer Soldiers" by Erika Ritter
in Saturday Night Magazine, June 1981.
Colored pencil and acrylic on board.

Steve Carver Artist
Steve Carver Designer
Janet Perr Art Director
Rolling Stone Publication
Straight Arrow, Inc. Publisher

Illustration for an article entitled "Exile on Pain Street"
by Stephen Holden, in Rolling Stone magazine, September 1981.
Acrylic.

Christine Bunn Artist
B.J. Galbraith Designer
B.J. Galbraith Art Director
Saturday Night Contract Publishing Publisher
Canadian Broadcasting Corporation Client

Cover illustration commemorating the one hundredth birthday
anniversary of James Joyce for CBC Radio Guide #3,
January 1982.
Colored pencils (prismacolor).

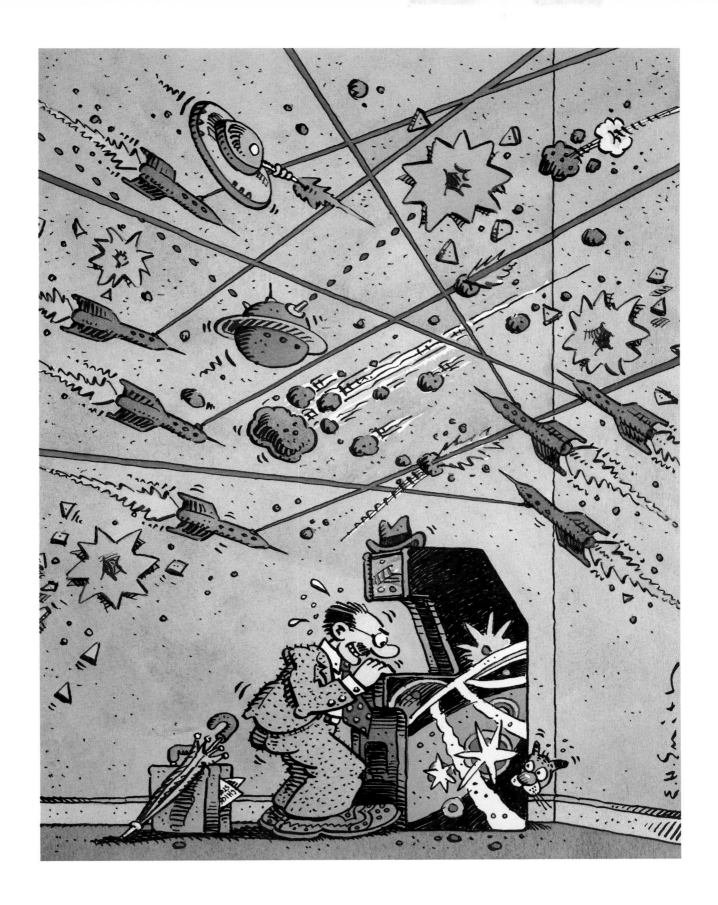

Elwood H. Smith Artist
April Silver Designer
Robert Priest Art Director
Esquire Publication
Esquire Publishing, Inc. Publisher

Color illustration for an article entitled "Invasion of the Asteroids" by
David Owen in Esquire magazine, February 1981.
Watercolor.

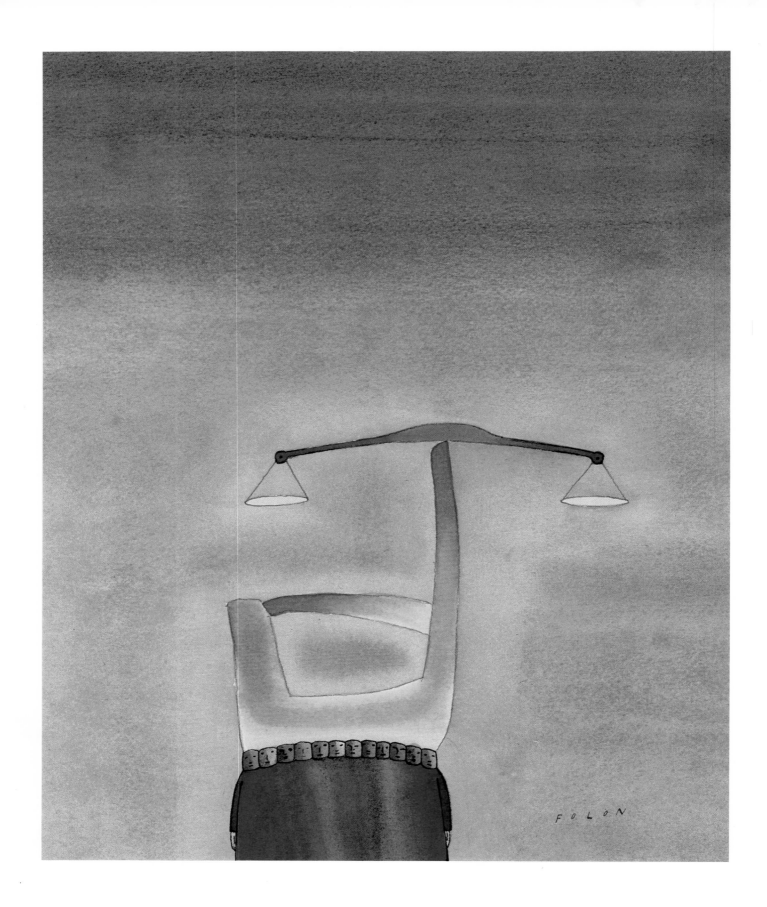

Jean Michel Folon Artist
Rudolph Hoglund Art Director
Time Magazine Publication
Time Inc. Publisher

Cover illustration for a feature entitled "We, the Jury"
by Otto Friedrich, September 28, 1981.
Watercolor.

Liz Pyle Artist
Chris Jones Art Director
New Scientist Publication
IPC Magazines Ltd. Publisher

Cover illustration for a feature entitled "Magnetism of the Earth—The
Past in Ancient Bricks" in New Scientist magazine,
June 11, 1981.
Pastel.

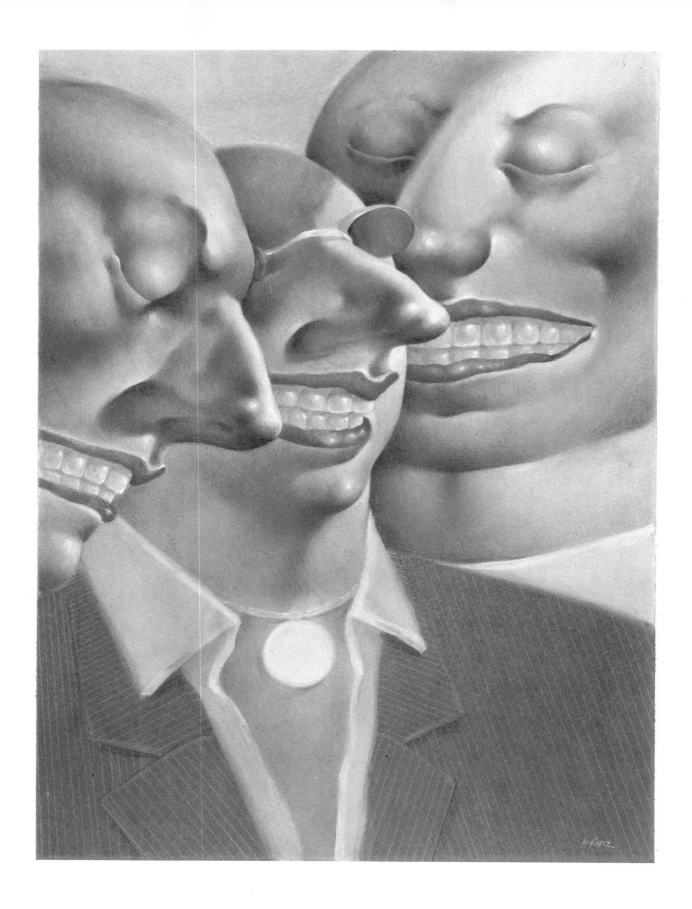

76, 77

Anita Kunz Artist
Bruce Ramsay Designer
Derek Ungless Art Director
Saturday Night Magazine Publication
Saturday Night Publications, Inc. Publisher

Illustration for an article entitled "The Conversion of the Jews" by Rick
Salutin in Saturday Night Magazine, January 1982.
Gouache and watercolor.

Seymour Chwast Artist
Judy Garlan Art Director
The Atlantic Monthly Publication
Atlantic Monthly Co. Publisher

Cover illustration for a feature article, "The Police and Neighborhood
Safety," in The Atlantic Monthly, March 1982.
Cello-tak.

Lynda Gray Artist
April Silver Designer
Robert Priest Art Director
Esquire Publication
Esquire Publishing, Inc. Publisher

Illustration for an article entitled "Shopgirls" by Frederick Barthelme
in Esquire magazine, January 1981.
Gouache.

Dagmar Frinta Artist
Greg Paul Art Director
Lisa Gitlin Writer
The Plain Dealer Magazine Publication
The Plain Dealer Publishing Co. Publisher

Illustration for an article entitled "Transsexuals" by Lisa Gitlin
published in The Plain Dealer Magazine, February 14, 1982.
Watercolor and mixed media.

Seymour Chwast Artist
Christopher Austopchuk Art Director
Rolling Stone Publication
Straight Arrow, Inc. Publisher

Illustration for a review of an Elvis Costello
album in Rolling Stone magazine, March 1981.
Pastel.

82, 83

Blair Drawson Artist
Mary Opper Designer
Derek Ungless Art Director
Saturday Night Magazine Publication
Saturday Night Publications, Inc. Publisher

Series of illustrations for an article entitled
"The Homosexual Factor" by Paul Delaney in
Saturday Night Magazine, February 1981.
Watercolor.

David Suter Artist
Nigel Holmes Designer
Rudolph Hoglund and Nigel Holmes Art Directors
Time Magazine Publication
Time Inc. Publisher

Cover illustration for a feature entitled "Embattled Britain" by
Marguerite Johnson, February 1981.
Colored pencil.

85

Sue Coe Artist
Mary Opper Designer
Derek Ungless Art Director
Saturday Night Magazine Publication
Saturday Night Publications, Inc. Publisher

Full-page illustration for an article entitled
"The Decline in Public Morality" by Dalton Camp
in Saturday Night Magazine, January 1981.
Acrylic and mixed media.

Jamie Hogan Artist
Ronn Campisi Designer
Ronn Campisi Art Director
The Boston Globe Magazine Publication
Globe Newspaper Co. Publisher

Cover illustration for a feature entitled
"Gold in the Ring—The Big Money in Professional
Boxing" by Steve Marantz in The Boston Globe Magazine,
September 13, 1981.
Gouache, charcoal and pastel.

87

James McMullan Artist
Ellen Rongstad Designer
Robert Priest Art Director
Esquire Publication
Esquire Publishing, Inc. Publisher

Illustration for an article entitled "Catcher Comes of Age"
by Adam Moss in Esquire magazine, December 1981.
Watercolor.

Sandra Dionisi Artist
James Ireland Consulting Art Director
Barbara Solowan Art Director
Toronto Life Magazine Publication
Key Publishers Publisher

Illustration for an article on Oscar Peterson
by Gene Lees in Toronto Life Magazine, September 1981.
Watercolor.

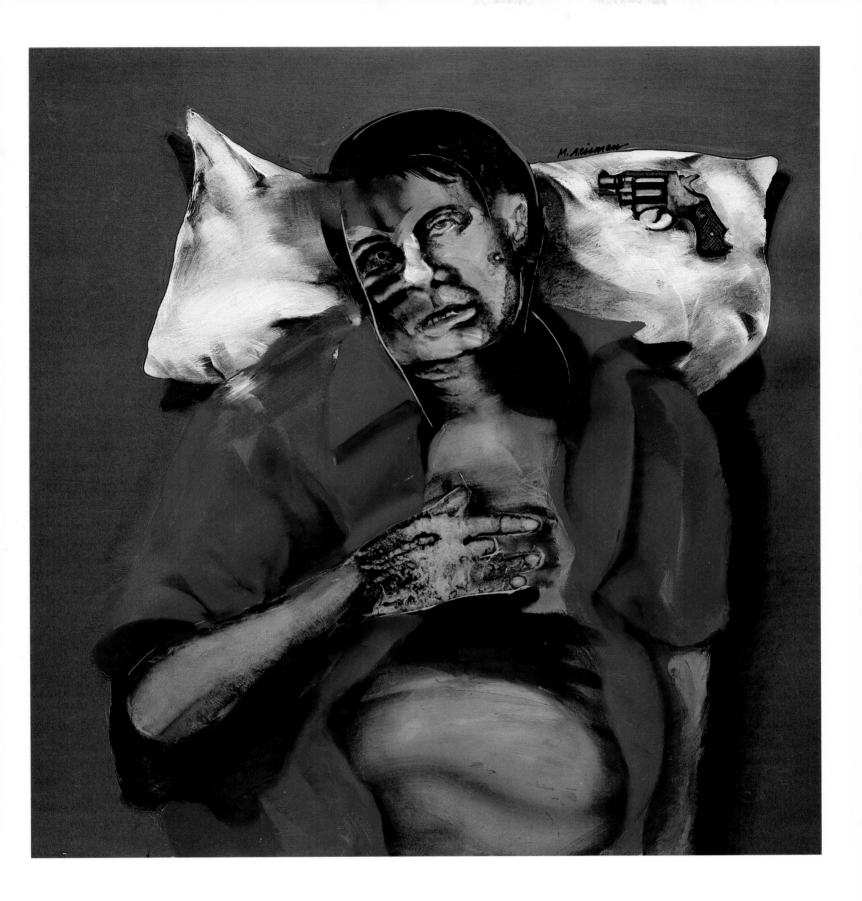

Marshall Arisman Artist
Claire Victor Designer
Joe Brooks Art Director
Penthouse Publication
Penthouse International Ltd. Publisher

Illustration for an article entitled "Our Father Who Art in Hell"
by James Reston, Jr., in Penthouse magazine, May 1981.
Oil on paper.

James McMullan Artist
James McMullan Designer
Walter Herdeg Art Editor
Graphis Publication
Graphis Press Corp. Publisher

Cover illustration for Graphis magazine's Spring 1982 issue containing
feature article about the artist.
Watercolor.

91

Guy Billout Artist
Judy Garlan Art Director
The Atlantic Monthly Publication
Atlantic Monthly Co. Publisher

Cover illustration for a feature article,
"The Last of the Pure Baseball Men," by Michael Leneman
in The Atlantic Monthly magazine, August 1981.
Watercolor.

Guy Billout Artist
Judy Garlan Art Director
The Atlantic Monthly Publication
Atlantic Monthly Co. Publisher

Full-page drawing entitled "Detour" published in
The Atlantic Monthly magazine, February 1982.
Watercolor.

93
Guy Billout Artist
Judy Garlan Art Director
The Atlantic Monthly Publication
Atlantic Monthly Co. Publisher

Full-page drawing entitled "Intersection" published
in The Atlantic Monthly magazine, April 1982.
Watercolor.

94

Ralph Steadman Artist
Claire Victor Designer
Joe Brooks Art Director
Penthouse Publication
Penthouse International Ltd. Publisher

Illustration for an article entitled "The President's Men:
William French Smith" by Jeff Stein in Penthouse, August 1981.
Pen and ink and gouache.

YANKS
GO
HOME

Ralph Steadman Artist
Claire Victor Designer
Joe Brooks Art Director
Penthouse Publication
Penthouse International Ltd. Publisher

Illustration for an article entitled "The President's Men:
Alexander Haig" by Jeff Stein in Penthouse magazine, June 1981.
Pen and ink and gouache.

Elwood H. Smith Artist
Bill Kobasz Art Director
School of Visual Arts Press Inc. Advertising Agency
Raw Publication
School of Visual Arts Client

Promotional piece for School of Visual Arts in Raw magazine, 1982.
Watercolor.

97

Blair Drawson Artist
April Silver Designer
Robert Priest Art Director
Esquire Publication
Esquire Publishing, Inc. Publisher

Illustration for an article entitled "The Ghost Soldiers"
by Tim O'Brien in Esquire magazine, March 1981.
Ink and watercolor.

98

Vivienne Flesher Artist
Steve Heller Designer
Steve Heller Art Director
The New York Times Publisher

B&W illustrations for an article entitled "Victory in Europe"
by Drew Middleton in The New York Times
Book Review Section, June 28, 1981.
Charcoal.

Doug Smith Artist
Catherine Aldrich Designer
Ronn Campisi Art Director
The Boston Globe Magazine Publication
Globe Newspaper Co. Publisher

B&W illustration for a story entitled
"Fired Up Over Wild Duck" by Wendy Quinones in The Boston Globe
Magazine, November 8, 1981.
Scratchboard.

JEFFREY J. SMITH,

100

Jeffrey J. Smith Artist
Sherri Thompson Art Director
Songwriter Publication

Color portrait for "John Lennon: A Tribute"
in Songwriter magazine, January 1981.
Watercolor and gouache.

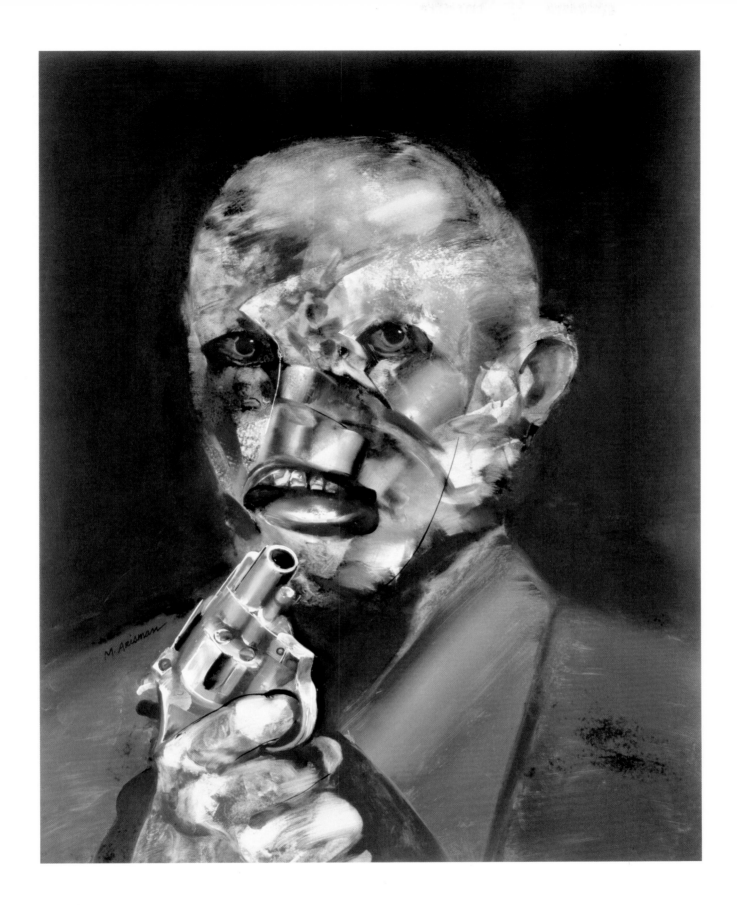

Marshall Arisman Artist
Rudolph Hoglund Art Director
Time Magazine Publication
Time Inc. Publisher

Cover illustration for a feature article entitled "The Curse of Violent
Crime" by Edward Magnuson, March 23, 1981.
Oil on rag paper.

102

Henrik Drescher Artist
Lynn Staley Designer
Lynn Staley Art Director
The Boston Globe Magazine Publication
Globe Newspaper Co. Publisher

Illustration for "Miniatures," a story by Marya Dantzer-Rosenthal
in The Boston Globe Magazine, January 7, 1982.
Pencil and ink.

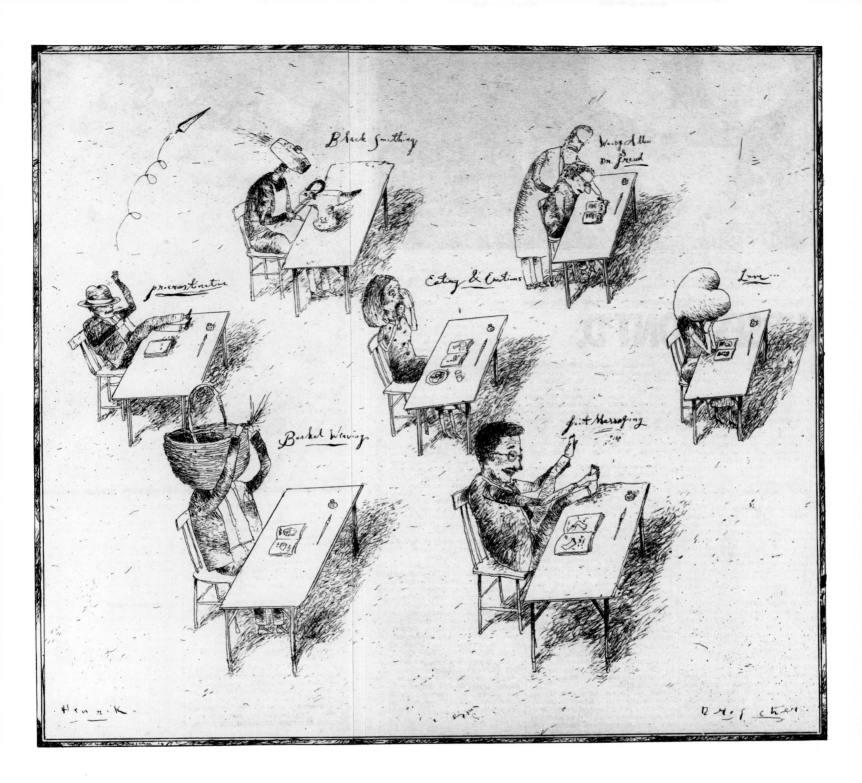

103

Henrik Drescher Artist
Lynn Staley Designer
Lynn Staley Art Director
The Boston Globe Magazine Publication
Globe Newspaper Co. Publisher

B&W illustration for an article entitled "Krazy Kourses" by Gerald
Peary in The Boston Globe Magazine, August 27, 1981.
Ink.

David Wilcox Artist
Claire Victor Designer
Joe Brooks Art Director
Penthouse Publication
Penthouse International Ltd. Publisher

Illustration for an article entitled "The Adolf Hitler Fast Food
Franchise" by Nick Tosches in Penthouse magazine, March 1981.
Acrylic.

Janet Woolley Artist
Stephen Doyle Designer
Stephen Doyle Art Director
Rolling Stone Publication
Straight Arrow, Inc. Publisher

Illustration for a record review of British synthesizer groups,
"Electronic Pop: The Latest Rage in Britain," by David Fricke.
Published in Rolling Stone magazine, May 13, 1982.
Mixed media.

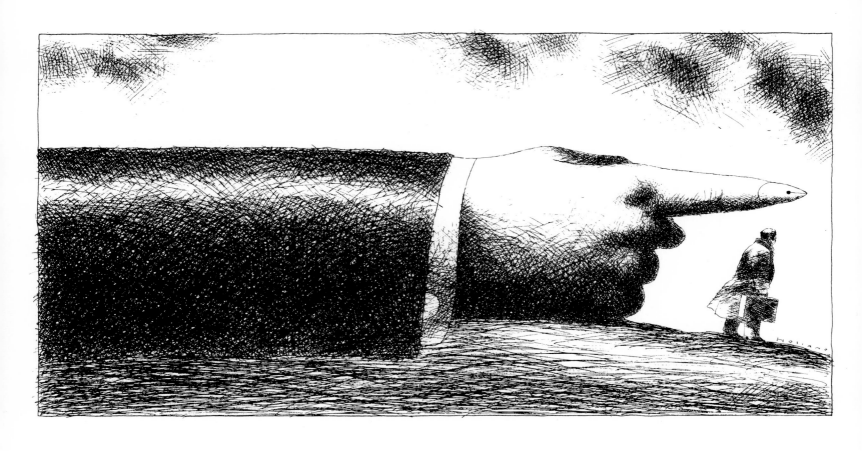

Brad Holland Artist
Greg Paul Art Director
Charles Greenfield Writer
The Plain Dealer Magazine Publication
The Plain Dealer Publishing Co. Publisher

B&W illustration for an article entitled
"Cuban Writers in Exile" by Charles Greenfield
published in The Plain Dealer Magazine, April 26, 1981.
Pen and ink.

Brad Holland Artist
Greg Paul Art Director
Tom Wolfe Author
The Plain Dealer Magazine Publication
The Plain Dealer Publishing Co. Publisher

Illustration for an excerpt of the book *From Bauhaus to Our House* by
Tom Wolfe, in The Plain Dealer Magazine, August 2, 1981.
Pen and ink.

108,109

Liz Pyle Artist
Caroline Bowyer Designer
Caroline Bowyer Art Director
Book Digest Publication
Dow Jones & Company, Inc. Publisher

Illustrations for an article entitled "The Soul of a New Machine"
by Tracy Kidder published in Book Digest magazine, January 1982.
Pastel.

Philip Burke Artist
Philip Burke and Stephen Kroninger Designers
Philip Burke and Stephen Kroninger Art Directors
Meat Publication

One of a series of satiric drawings for an
independent publication called Meat, Summer 1982.
Pen and ink.

111

Henrik Drescher Artist
Ronn Campisi Designer
Ronn Campisi Art Director
The Boston Globe Magazine Publication
Globe Newspaper Co. Publisher

B&W illustration for an article entitled
"Fueling New England's Future" by John Tirman
in The Boston Globe Magazine, November 29, 1981.
Pen and ink and wash.

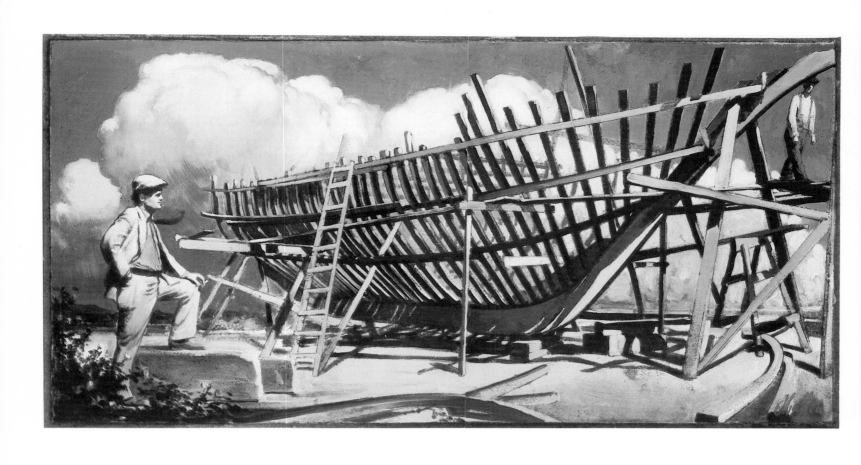

Daniel Maffia Artist
B. Martin Pedersen Designer
B. Martin Pedersen Art Director
Nautical Quarterly Publication
Nautical Quarterly Co. Publisher

Illustration for an article entitled "The Inconceivable and Monstrous"
by Jack London in Nautical Quarterly 16, Winter 1981.
Oil.

Liz Pyle Artist
Mary Opper Designer
Derek Ungless Art Director
Saturday Night Magazine Publication
Saturday Night Publications, Inc. Publisher

Illustration for a poem entitled "Digging In" by Elizabeth Brewster
published in Saturday Night Magazine, May 1981.
Colored crayons.

Dennis Noble Artist
Ken Rodmell Art Director
Toronto Life Magazine Publication
Key Publishers Publisher

B&W illustration for an article entitled "Kazmer's Burden" by George
Jonas in Toronto Life Magazine, September 1981.
Acrylic.

115

Vivienne Flesher Artist
Ronn Campisi Designer
Ronn Campisi Art Director
The Boston Globe Magazine Publication
Globe Newspaper Co. Publisher

B&W illustration for "Radical Love," a fiction article
by Fanny Howe in The Boston Globe Magazine, August 1981.
Pastel.

116

John Craig Artist
Theo Kouvatsos Designer
Tom Staebler Art Director
Playboy Publication
Playboy Enterprises, Inc. Publisher

Illustration for an article entitled "Inside the New Right War Machine"
by Peter Ross Range in Playboy magazine, August 1981.
Mixed media.

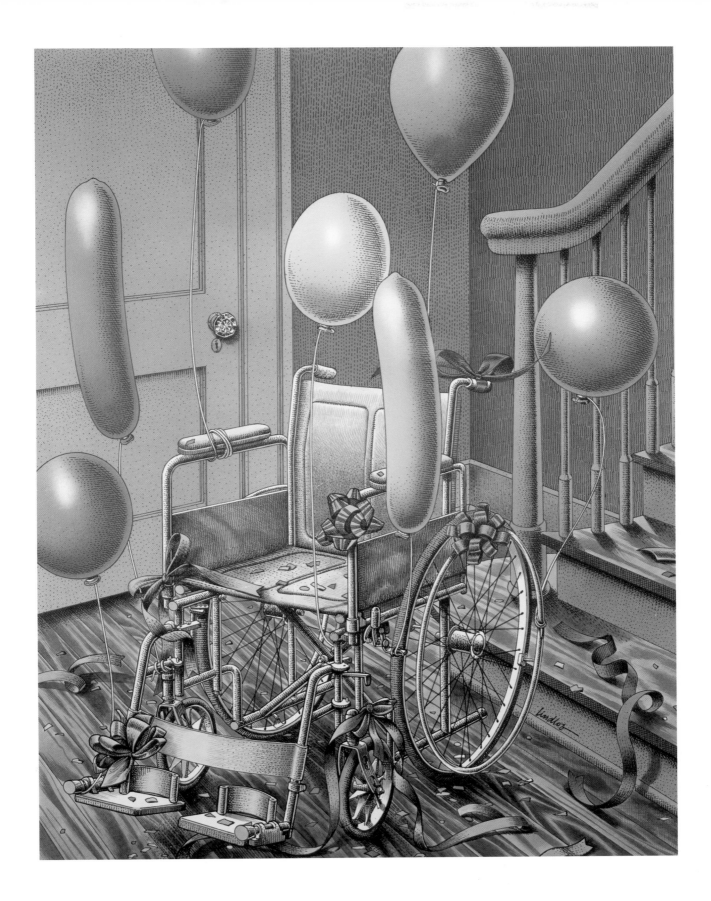

Ed Lindlof Artist
Tamara Schnieder Designer
Tamara Schnieder Art Director
Seventeen Publication
Triangle Communications, Inc. Publisher

Illustration for an article entitled "Missy"
by Lois Anne Naylor in Seventeen magazine, October 1981.
India ink and colored inks.

Mark Marek Artist
National Lampoon Publication
NL Communications, Inc. Publisher

B&W illustration for Funny Pages Section
of National Lampoon magazine, November 1981.
Ink, acrylic and collage.

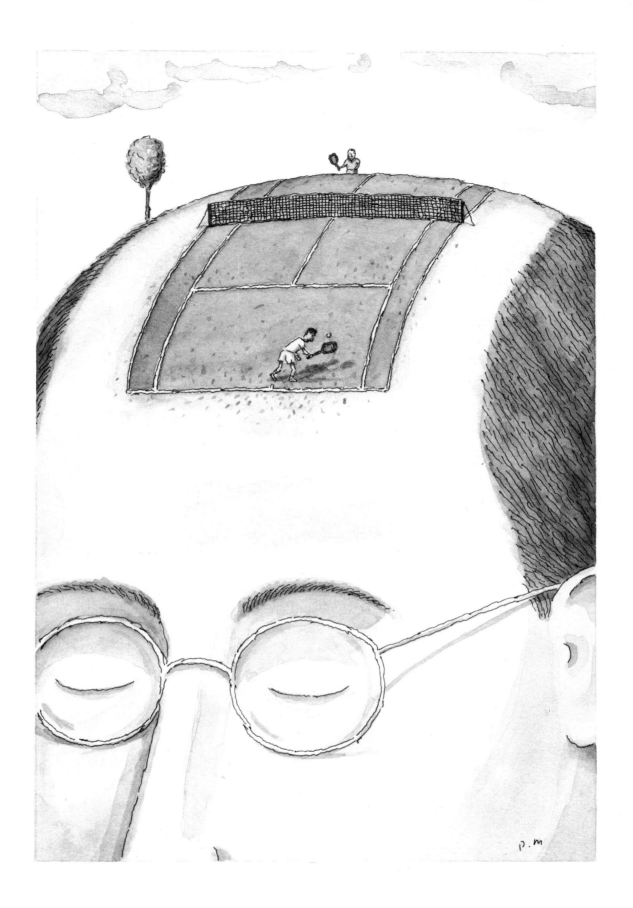

Paul Meisel Artist
Andrea Da Rif Designer
Andrea Da Rif Art Director
Racquet Quarterly Publication
Heather & Pine International, Inc. Publisher

B&W drawing from an artist's portfolio entitled "The Tennis Player—
A Creative Portfolio of Humorous, Satirical and Transcendental
Interpretations" published in Racquet Quarterly magazine, Spring
1982.
Pen and ink and watercolor.

120, 121

Donna Muir Artist
Art Niemi Designer
Stephen Costello Art Director
Quest Publication
Comac Communications Ltd. Publisher

Three of a series of illustrations for an article entitled "An American
Odyssey" by Jack MacLeod in Quest magazine,
March 1982.
Color xerography, watercolor and pastel.

122

Vivienne Flesher Artist
Lynn Staley Designer
Lynn Staley Art Director
The Boston Globe Magazine Publication
Globe Newspaper Co. Publisher

B&W illustration for an article on Woody Allen
in The Boston Globe Magazine, January 14, 1982.
Charcoal.

123

Seymour Chwast Artist
Jerelle Kraus Designer
Jerelle Kraus Art Director
The New York Times Publisher

B&W illustration for Op-Ed Page
of The New York Times, September 24, 1981.
Ink.

Joel Resnicoff Artist
Joel Resnicoff Designer
Bruce Fitzgerald Art Director
Luxe Publication
Woodhill Press Publisher

Illustration for an article entitled "Portrait of a Young Man"
by Bob Smith in Luxe magazine, May 1, 1981.
Gouache and charcoal.

125

Patricia Dryden Artist
Janet Perr Designer
Janet Perr Art Director
Rolling Stone Publication
Straight Arrow, Inc. Publisher

Illustration for a record review, "Lou Reed: The Blue Mask," by Tom
Carson published in Rolling Stone magazine, April 15, 1982.
Pastel.

126, 127

Harvey Dinnerstein Artist
Judy Garlan Designer
Judy Garlan Art Director
The Atlantic Monthly Publication
Atlantic Monthly Co. Publisher

B&W illustrations for "The Kingdom of Auschwitz"
by Otto Friedrich in The Atlantic Monthly, September 1981.
Charcoal and pastel.

Paola Piglia Artist
Karen Klingon Designer
Susan Niles Art Director
Self Publication
The Condé Nast Publications, Inc. Publisher

Illustration for an article entitled "Part-time Insomniacs"
by Denise M. Topolnicki in Self magazine, December 1981.
Watercolor.

129

Mel Odom Artist
Kerig Pope Designer
Tom Staebler Art Director
Playboy Publication
Playboy Enterprises, Inc. Publisher

Illustration for an article entitled "The New Tattoo"
by Robert Cole in Playboy magazine, June 1981.
Watercolor.

Dagmar Frinta Artist
Greg Paul Designer
Greg Paul Art Director
The Plain Dealer Publication
The Plain Dealer Publishing Co. Publisher

Illustration for "The Nutcracker Story"
by E.T.A. Hoffman published in
The Plain Dealer Magazine, November 1981.
Mixed media.

Alexa Grace Artist
Ronn Campisi Designer
Ronn Campisi Art Director
The Boston Globe Magazine Publication
Globe Newspaper Co. Publisher

Illustration to depict a certain woman who can fix anything, published
in The Boston Globe Magazine's Getting Around Section.
Watercolor and colored pencil.

Robert Grossman Artist
Rudolph Hoglund Designer
Rudolph Hoglund Art Director
Time Magazine Publication
Time Inc. Publisher

"Reagan in Choppy Waters" illustration for an article
by Charles Alexander in Time Magazine, September 21, 1981.
Watercolor.

133

Marshall Arisman Artist
Claire Victor Designer
Joe Brooks Art Director
Penthouse Publication
Penthouse International Ltd. Publisher

Illustration for an article entitled "The Park is Mine"
by Stephen Peters in Penthouse magazine, August 1981.
Oil on canvas.

Dennis Ziemienski Artist
Howard Shintaku Art Director
San Jose Mercury News/California Today Publication

Color illustration for an article entitled "Polo Politics at the Pink
Palace" by Barbara Grizzuti Harrison in San Jose
Mercury News/California Today, March 1981.
Acrylic.

Teresa Fasolino Artist
Ellen Rongstad Designer
Robert Priest Art Director
Esquire Publication
Esquire Publishing, Inc. Publisher

Illustration for an article entitled "The Trouble with Harvard"
by Timothy Foote in Esquire magazine, September 1981.
Acrylic.

Roman Balicki Artist
Bruce Ramsay Designer
Derek Ungless Art Director
Saturday Night Magazine Publication
Saturday Night Publications, Inc. Publisher

Illustration for an article entitled "The Honeymoon"
by Phil Murphy in Saturday Night Magazine, May 1982.
Colored pencil.

Scott Reynolds Artist
Pat Garling Art Director
Genesis Publication
Cycle Guide Publishing Co. Publisher

Illustration for an article entitled "Big Bertha"
in Genesis magazine, September 1980.
Pastel and spray paint.

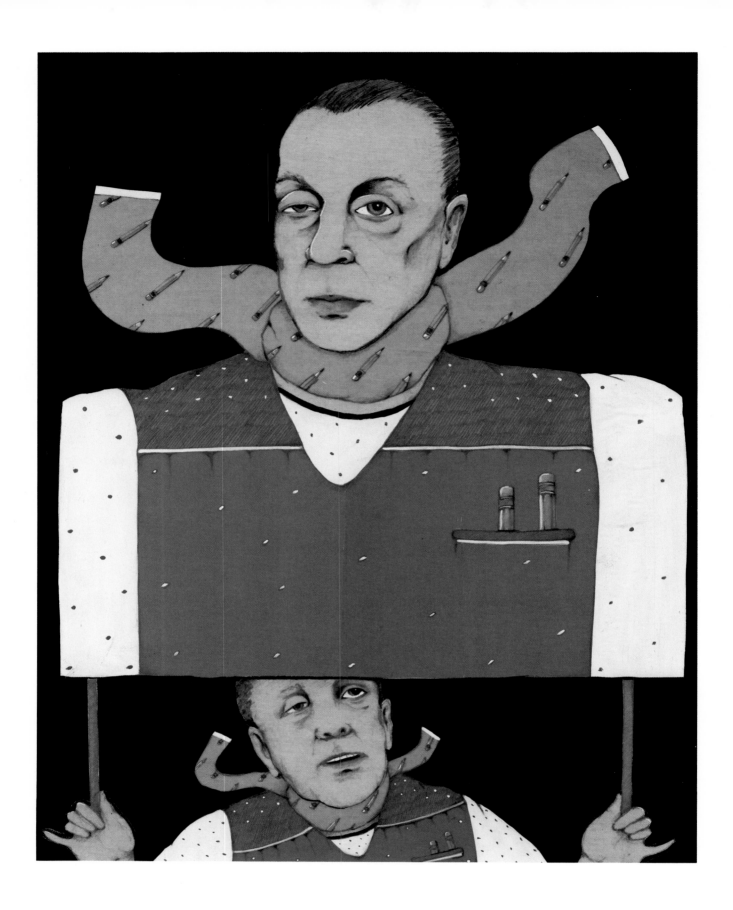

138,139
Dagmar Frinta Artist
Caroline Bowyer Designer
Caroline Bowyer Art Director
Book Digest Publication
Dow Jones & Company, Inc. Publisher

Series of illustrations for "The Mind's I," a collection of short stories by
Jorge Luis Borges, Terrel Miedaner and Daniel Dennett in Book Digest
magazine, March 1982.
Watercolor on blueprint paper.
Mixed media.

Richard Mantel Artist
Richard Mantel Designer
Seymour Chwast Art Director
Push Pin Graphic Publication
Push Pin Graphic, Inc. Publisher

"Going to Hell" cover illustration
for Push Pin Graphic magazine, February 1980.
Acrylic.

Paola Piglia Artist
April Silver Designer
Robert Priest Art Director
Esquire Publication
Esquire Publishing, Inc. Publisher

Illustration for an article entitled "The Enthusiast"
by Geoffrey Norman in Esquire magazine, June 1981.
Watercolor and crayons.

142

Alexa Grace Artist
Judy Garlan Designer
Judy Garlan Art Director
The Atlantic Monthly Publication
Atlantic Monthly Co. Publisher

One of a series of illustrations for a short story
entitled "Playing Trombone" by Nicholson Baker
in The Atlantic Monthly, March 1982.
Watercolor, pastel and pencil.

Blair Drawson Artist
Stephen Costello Designer
Stephen Costello Art Director
Quest Publication
Comac Communications Ltd. Publisher

Illustration for an article entitled "What Ever Happened to Good
Manners?" by John Lownsbrough in Quest magazine, June 1981.
Watercolor.

144

James Tughan Artist
James Tughan Designer
Jackie Young Art Director
The Financial Post Magazine Publication

Illustration for an article entitled "Best Sellers"
in The Financial Post Magazine, February 1982.
Chalk pastel and carbon pencil.

Ian Pollock Artist
April Silver Designer
Robert Priest Art Director
Esquire Publication
Esquire Publishing, Inc. Publisher

Illustration for a feature on Marlon Brando
in Esquire magazine, July 1981.
Watercolor.

Roman Balicki Artist
Roman Balicki Designer
Brad McIver Art Director
John Mackay Art Editor
Toronto Life Magazine Publication
Key Publishers Publisher

Illustrations for an article entitled "Beauty—The New Color Focus" by
Jane Mussett in Toronto Life Magazine, Spring 1982.
Black ink and make-up.

Renee Klein Artist
Ronn Campisi Art Director
The Boston Globe Magazine Publication
Globe Newspaper Co. Publisher

"Give Them Violence" illustration for an article by Michael Blowen in
The Boston Globe Magazine, August 19, 1979.
Pen and ink with cello-tak.

Christine Bunn Artist
Mary Opper Designer
Derek Ungless Art Director
Saturday Night Magazine Publication
Saturday Night Publications, Inc. Publisher

Illustration for "Ted's Wife" by Audrey Thomas, a fiction piece
published in Saturday Night Magazine, April 1981.
Colored pencil on board.

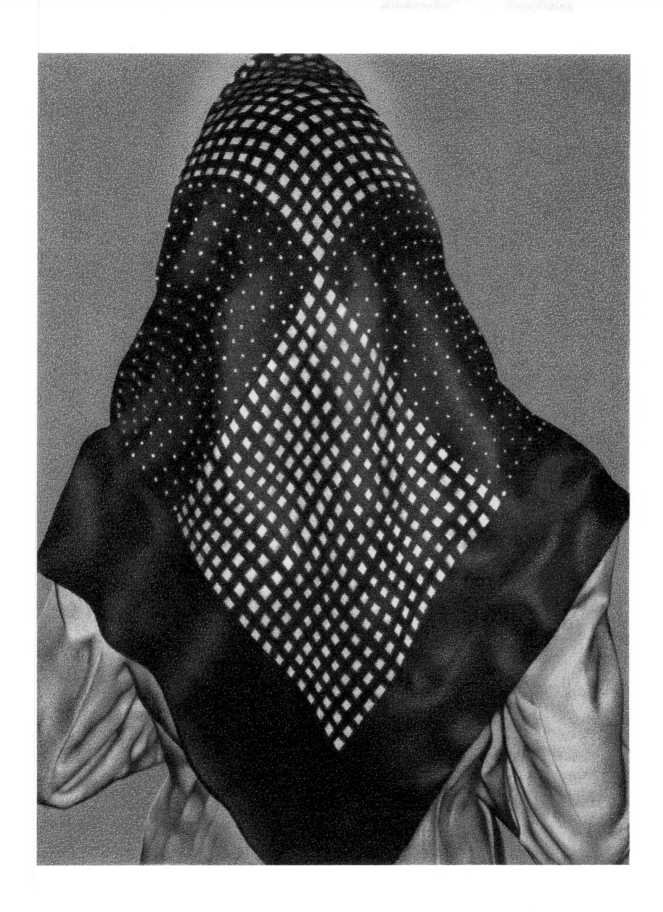

149

Christine Bunn Artist
Bruce Ramsay Designer
Derek Ungless Art Director
Saturday Night Magazine Publication
Saturday Night Publications, Inc. Publisher

Illustration for an article entitled "The Benefactor"
by Robertson Davies in Saturday Night Magazine, September 1981.
Colored pencil on board.

Seymour Chwast Artist
Judy Garlan Designer
Judy Garlan Art Director
The Atlantic Monthly Publication
Atlantic Monthly Co. Publisher

Illustration for a short story entitled "The Overcoat II"
by T. Coraghessan Boyle in The Atlantic Monthly, January 1982.
Acrylic and colored pencils on chipboard.

151

Richard Mantel Artist
Richard Mantel Designer
Seymour Chwast Art Director
Push Pin Graphic Publication
Push Pin Graphic, Inc. Publisher

Illustration for an article on the book
Imaginary Beings by Jorge Luis Borges
in Push Pin Graphic magazine, April 1980.
Acrylic.

152

Daniel Maffia Artist
B. Martin Pedersen Designer
B. Martin Pedersen Art Director
Nautical Quarterly Publication
Nautical Quarterly Co. Publisher

Illustration for an article entitled "The Inconceivable and Monstrous"
by Jack London in Nautical Quarterly 16, Winter 1981.
Oil.

153

Thomas Woodruff Artist
April Silver Designer
Robert Priest Art Director
Esquire Publication
Esquire Publishing, Inc. Publisher

Illustration for an article entitled "Breakfast"
by Joy Williams in Esquire magazine, August 1981.
Watercolor.

154

Braldt Bralds Artist
Braldt Bralds Designer
Michael Brock Art Director
Oui Magazine Publication
Laurant Publishing Ltd. Publisher

One of a series of illustrations for an interview series entitled
"One Woman" in Oui Magazine, August 1981.
Oil on masonite board.

155

Gary Panter Artist
Françoise Mouly & Art Spiegelman Designers
Françoise Mouly & Art Spiegelman Art Directors
Raw Publication
Raw Books & Graphics Inc. Publisher

Cover illustration for Raw magazine, Spring 1981.
Ink and mechanical color.

156

Marshall Arisman Artist
Bruce Ramsay Designer
Derek Ungless Art Director
Saturday Night Magazine Publication
Saturday Night Publications, Inc. Publisher

Cover illustration for a feature article entitled "The Unfriendly Giant"
by Viv Nelles in Saturday Night Magazine, February 1982.
Oil on paper.

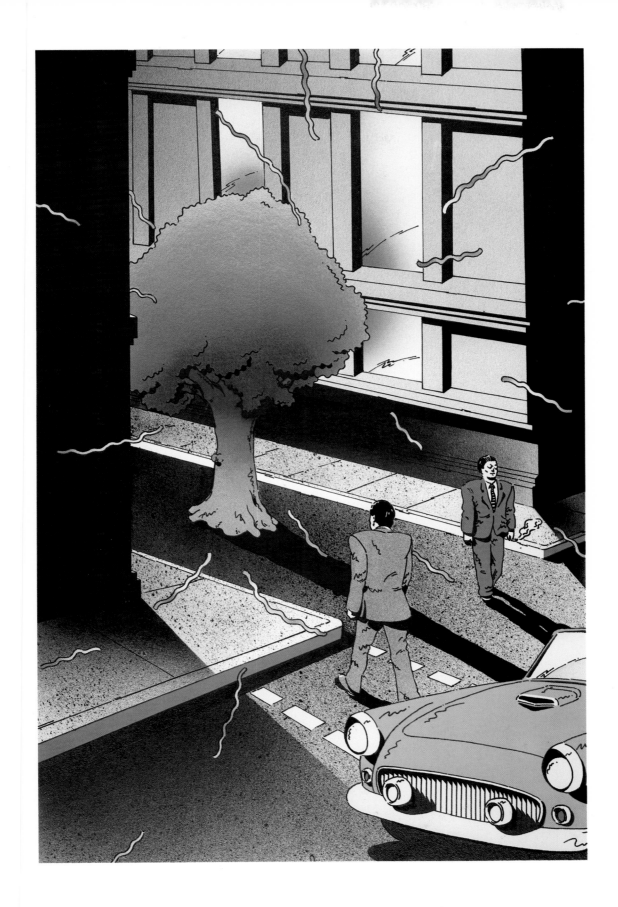

157

Terry Allen Artist
Catherine Aldrich Designer
Ronn Campisi Art Director and Chief Designer
The Boston Globe Magazine Publication
Globe Newspaper Co. Publisher

Illustration for an article entitled "Urban Greenery" by Catharine
Osgood Foster in The Boston Globe Magazine, January 1981.
Pen and ink with airbrush.

Jamie Hogan Artist
Ronn Campisi Designer
Ronn Campisi Art Director
The Boston Globe Magazine Publication
Globe Newspaper Co. Publisher

Cover illustration for a feature entitled "Veterans in Trouble"
by Michael D'Antonio in The Boston Globe Magazine, May 10, 1981.
Gouache, charcoal and pastel.

159

Vivienne Flesher Artist
Catherine Aldrich Designer
Ronn Campisi Art Director
The Boston Globe Magazine Publication
Globe Newspaper Co. Publisher

Portrait of James Joyce for a story on his works
written by Mopsy Strange Kennedy in The Boston Globe Magazine,
May 31, 1981.
Pastel.

Sue Llewellyn Artist
Science Digest Publication
The Hearst Corp. Publisher

Illustration for an article about physicists
published in Science Digest, July 1982.
Watercolor.

Books

This section includes work commissioned for book jackets, paperback covers, and all types of illustrated books, fiction and non-fiction.

162

Braldt Bralds Artist
Lidia Ferrara Art Director
Cecelia Holland Author
Alfred A. Knopf, Inc. Publisher

Book jacket illustration for *The Sea Beggars*
by Cecelia Holland, published May 1982.
Oil.

163, 164, 165

Sara Midda Artist
Sara Midda Designer
Paul Hansen Art Director
Sara Midda Author
Workman Publishing Co. Publisher

Illustrations from a book by the artist on garden lore entitled
In and Out of the Garden, published October 1981.
Watercolor.

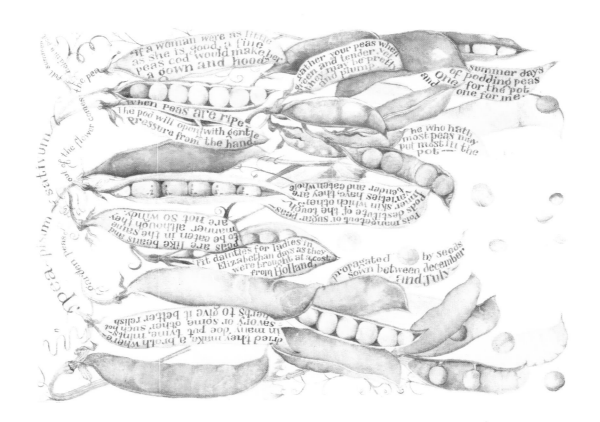

If a woman were as little as she is good, a fine peas cod would make her a gown and hood.

gather your peas when green and tender, very they may be pretty and plump

summer days of podding peas one for the pot and one for me.

when peas are ripe the pod will open with gentle pressure from the hand

he who hath most peas may put most in the pot — the

varieties have they ... tender and eaten whole Pods desirable or the tough inner skin which other... Peas mangetout or sugar peas

peas are like beans and to be eaten in the same manner although her ... are not so windy

Fit dainties for ladies in Elizabethan days as they were brought at a cost from Holland

propagated ... by seeds sown between december and July

dried they make a broth what ... in many, doe put tyme, mints, savory or some other such herbs to give it better relish

Pisum sativum — garden pea

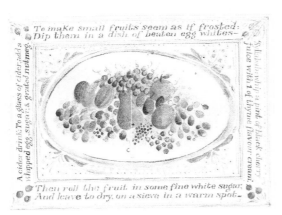

To make small fruits seem as if frosted: Dip them in a dish of beaten egg whites—

Then roll the fruit in some fine white sugar, And leave to dry on a sieve in a warm spot—

A cider drink To a glass of cider add a whipped egg, sugar & grated nutmeg.

Shrub: whip a pint of black cherry juice with 1 qt of thyme flavour cream.

Whole Strawberry Jam: Pick fine strawberries. To one pound of fruit allow ¾ pound of sugar. Cover sugar

with water, boil it into a clear syrup, drop the berries into this, and boil quickly, till the fruit is just cooked.

"Carrots are good to be eaten with salt-fish, therefore sow carrots in your gardens, and humbly praise God for them, as for a singular and great blessing; Admit if it should please God that any City or towne should be besieged with the Enemy, what better provision for the greatest number of people can be then every garden to be sufficiently planted with carrots?"
Richard Gardiner

CONTAINS 120 SEEDS

MIXED
Vegetables
ROOT

"If you would have parsnip, radish, turnip, carrot, etc. to have a large root, tread down the tops often, else the sap will run into the leaves."

Salsify or vegetable oyster said by Parkinson– "they make a pleasant dish of meat, far passing the parsnip in many mens judgements."

To put in a soup or tasty stew some wholesome roots for me and you.

A very ancient vegetable is the Skirret, thought to be a native of China. Though the roots are fiddling to clean, Elizabethans used them in pies, with eggs, artichoke bottoms, chestnuts, potatoes, dried fruit and spices.

green leaves of turnips can be used in salads, or boiled and eaten with salt meats

carrot – "honey underground"

carrot leaves in Charles I time were worn as an ornament by women in his court . .

"the parsnip affords by proper management, one of our best, cheapest and wholesomest home-made wines." R. Ellerman

166

Ed Lindlof Artist
Richard Hendel Designer
Richard Hendel Art Director
Joan D. Hedrick Author
University of North Carolina Press Publisher

Book jacket illustration for *Solitary Comrade*
by Joan D. Hedrick, published October 1981.
Brush and ink.

167

Lou Brooks Artist
Brad Benedict Art Director
Brad Benedict Author
Harmony Books Publisher

Book illustration for *Love—The Art of Romance* by Brad Benedict,
published January 1982.
Ink and airbrush.

168

Dagmar Frinta Artist
Louise Fili Designer
Louise Fili Art Director
Yashar Kemal Author
Pantheon Books, Inc. Publisher

Book jacket illustration for *Memed, My Hawk*
by Yashal Kemal, published March 1982.
Gouache.

169

Dagmar Frinta Artist
Louise Fili Designer
Louise Fili Art Director
Robert Musil Author
Pantheon Books, Inc. Publisher

Book jacket illustration for *Young Torless*
by Robert Musil, published March 1982.
Gouache.

170

Bascove Artist
Bascove Designer
Dick Adleson Art Director
Robertson Davies Author
The Viking Press Publisher

Cover illustration for a book entitled *The Rebel Angels*
by Robertson Davies, published 1981.
Woodcut and watercolor.

171

Patric Fourshé Artist
Patricia Candor Designer
Patricia Candor Art Director

Illustration for book jacket commissioned
by Right On Productions, 1980.
Casein and acrylic.

172,173

Steven Guarnaccia Artist
Steve Heller Designer
Steve Heller Art Director
Alfa-Betty Olsen and Marshall Efron Authors
A & W Publishers, Inc. Publisher

B&W book illustrations for *Sin City Fables* by Alfa-Betty Olsen and
Marshall Efron, published December 1980.
Pen and ink and watercolor.

174

Frank K. Morris Artist
Emily Prager & Frank Morris Authors
Pocket Books Publisher

Book illustration for *The Official I-Hate-Video Games Handbook*
by Emily Prager and Frank Morris.
Acrylic.

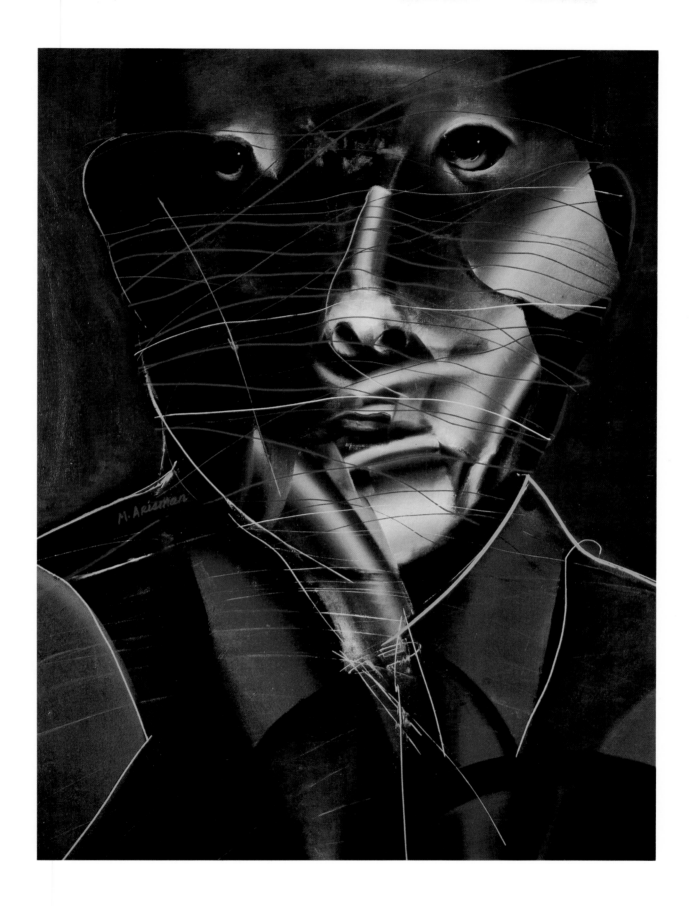

175

Marshall Arisman Artist
Louise Fili Designer
Louise Fili Art Director
Joel Kovel Author
Pantheon Books, Inc. Publisher

Book jacket illustration for *The Age of Desire*
by Joel Kovel, published January 1982.
Acrylic.

Amy Horowitz Artist
Louise Fili Designer
Louise Fili Art Director
Leonard Kriegel Author
Pantheon Books, Inc. Publisher

Book jacket illustration for *Quitting Time*,
a novel by Leonard Kriegel published March 1982.
Colored pencil.

DODO
Raphus cucullatus
30" tall   46 lbs
Extinct, ca. 1693

Dugald Stermer Artist
Dugald Stermer Designer
Dugald Stermer Art Director
Dugald Stermer Author
Lancaster-Miller Publishers Publisher

One of a series of illustrations of endangered and extinct creatures for a
book entitled *Vanishing Creatures*, published January 1981.
Pencil and watercolor.

Vivienne Flesher Artist
Louise Fili Designer
Louise Fili Art Designer
Nicholas Freeling Author
Pantheon Books, Inc. Publisher

Book jacket illustration for *Wolfnight*
by Nicholas Freeling, published April 1982.
Pastel.

179

Marvin Mattelson Artist
Patty Pecoraro Designer
Patty Pecoraro Art Director
Agatha Christie Author
Dell Publishing Co., Inc. Publisher

Book illustration for *Murder at the Hazelmoor*
by Agatha Christie, published Fall 1982.
Acrylic.

180, 181

Guy Billout Artist
Carl Barile Designer
Barbara Francis Art Director
Guy Billout Author
Prentice-Hall, Inc. Publisher

Book illustrations for *Thunderbolt and Rainbow* by Guy Billout,
published by Prentice-Hall, Inc. October 1981.
Watercolor.

Advertising

This section includes work commissioned for advertising in consumer, trade and professional magazines, and newspapers.

184

Doug Johnson Artist
George Grodzicki Art Director
Burlington Industries Client

Advertisement to promote worsted wool fabric with the slogan "Then
and Now Worsteds." Published in Women's Wear Daily in color,
October 1981.
Gouache.

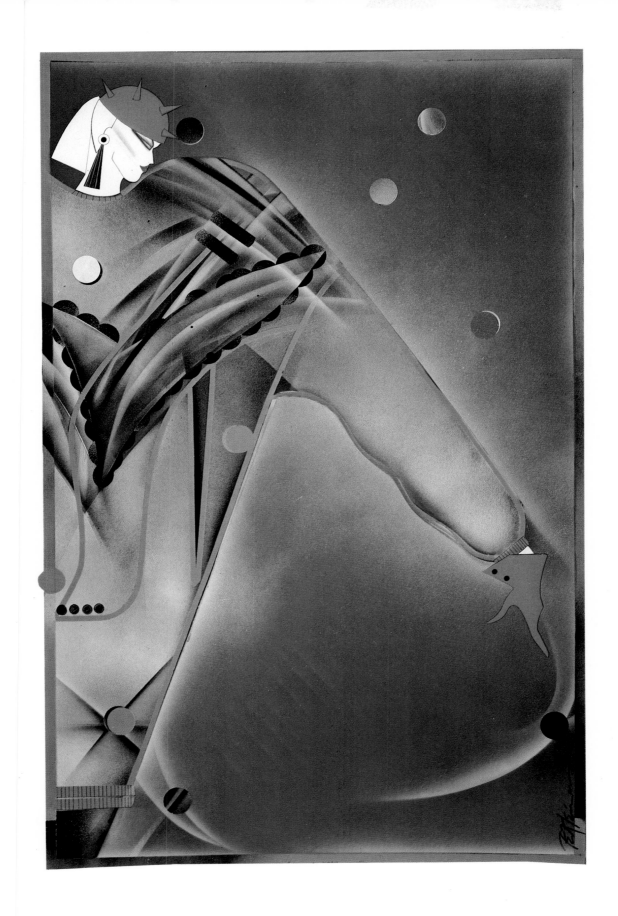

185

Jane Kleinman Artist
Dianne Benson Art Director

B&W and color advertisement for Dianne B. Boutique published in
Interview magazine, August 1981.
Spray paint, pastel and make-up.

David Wilcox Artist
Michael V. Phillips Art Director
Richard Jacobs Copywriter
Frank J. Corbett, Inc. (Division of BBDO) Advertising Agency
Breon Laboratories Client

Illustration to advertise the local anesthetic
Marcaine HCl in medical journals, with the copyline
"Up to 24 hours of Painlessness," April 1982.
Acrylic on masonite.

187

Richard Mantel Artist
Seymour Chwast Art Director
C.Q.S. Computerized Quality Separations Client

One of a series to advertise color separations for C.Q.S. Computerized
Quality Separations in Push Pin Graphic Magazine.
Colored paper and acrylic.

188, 189, 190

Dagmar Frinta Artist
Russell Patrick Art Director
Bob Chatain Copywriter
Graphic Solutions Advertising Agency
SONY Client

A series of portraits used in a brochure
to promote the "magic" of Trinitron televisions,
with the copyline "Think Trinitron," 1982.
Watercolor.

Posters

This section includes work commissioned
for posters, including consumer products
and institutional.

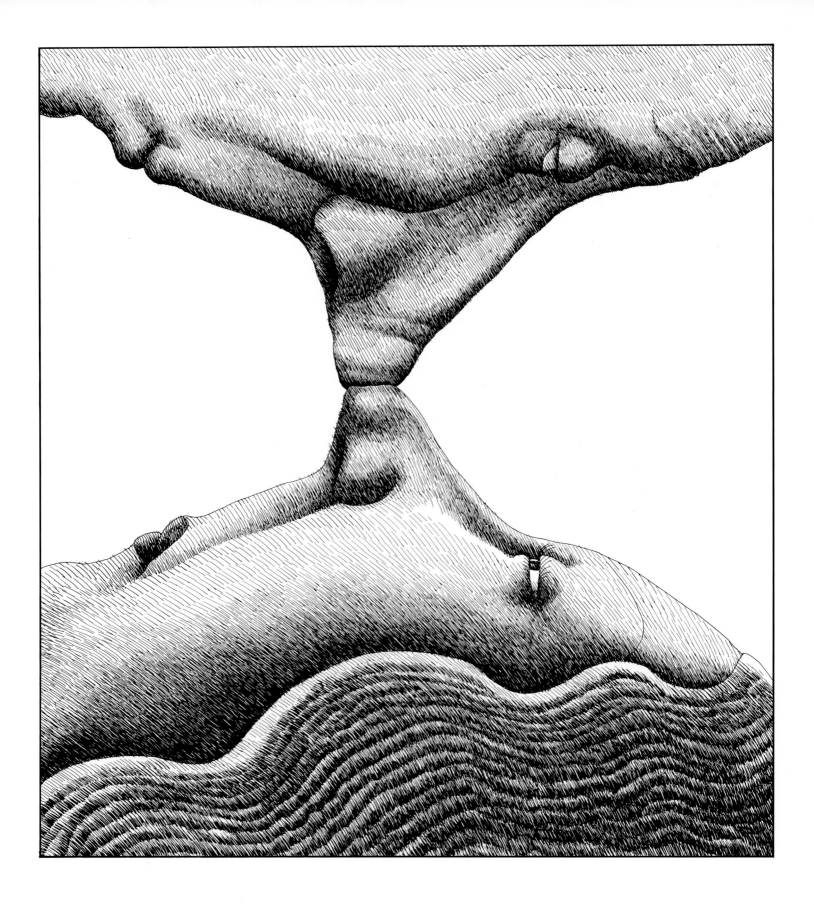

192

Fred Hilliard Artist
Fred Hilliard Art Director
Seattle Repertory Theatre Client

B&W poster for a play called Bedroom Farce with the copyline, "You
will tell me if you get bored, won't you?"
Pen and ink.

MUSEUM MILE 5TH AVE. NEW YORK

METROPOLITAN MUSEUM OF ART

GOETHE HOUSE

YIVO INSTITUTE FOR JEWISH RESEARCH

SOLOMON R. GUGGENHEIM MUSEUM

NATIONAL ACADEMY OF DESIGN

COOPER HEWITT MUSEUM

THE JEWISH MUSEUM

INTERNATIONAL CENTER OF PHOTOGRAPHY

MUSEUM OF THE CITY OF NEW YORK

EL MUSEO DEL BARRIO

193

R.O. Blechman Artist
Cynthia Schupf Art Director
Museum Mile Client

Poster to advertise museums along
upper Fifth Avenue in New York, Summer 1981.
Collage and watercolor.

194

Blair Drawson Artist
Louis Fishauf Art Director

Self-promotion poster.
Watercolor.

195

James McMullan Artist
James McMullan and Phil Hays Designers
Phil Hays Art Director
Art Center College of Design Publisher

Exhibition poster for one-man show, February 1982.
Watercolor.

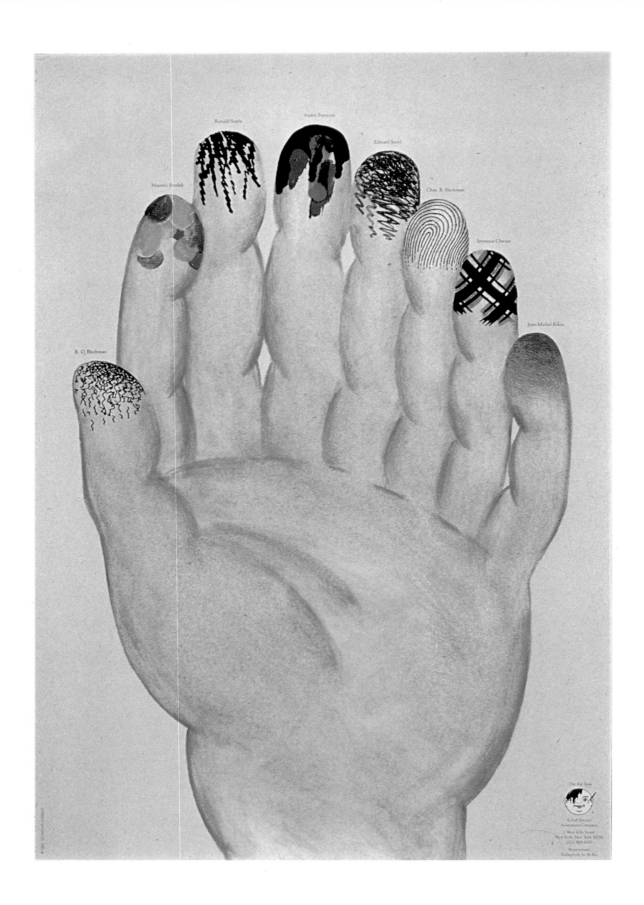

196

Seymour Chwast Artist
Seymour Chwast Art Director
Ink Tank Client

Poster to publicize Ink Tank animation studio.
Mixed media.

The Writer's New York City Source Book

City of New York
Edward I. Koch, Mayor
Department of Cultural Affairs
Henry Geldzahler, Commissioner
Arts Apprenticeship Program

197

Seymour Chwast Artist
Grey Advertising Advertising Agency
N.Y.C. Dept. of Cultural Affairs Client

Poster and book jacket to publicize The Writer's
New York City Source Book, December 1981.
Cello-tak.

198

Seymour Chwast Artist
Seymour Chwast Art Director
Push Pin Studios Client

Studio designed and produced poster for
distribution with the copyline "Carta Di Pasta."
Cello-tak.

199

Edward Sorel Artist
Edward Sorel Art Director
L'Affiche Gallerie Ltd. Advertising Agency
Liberty House Hawaii Client

Poster with the copyline "New York, New York"
to advertise Liberty House Department Store
in Hawaii.
Pen and ink and watercolor.

Doug Johnson Artist
Doug Johnson and Anne Leigh Art Directors

Self-promotion poster, 1981.
Gouache.

Barbara Nessim Artist
Shinichiro Tora Art Director
Dai Nippon Printing Advertising Agency
Japan Hotel Barman Association Client

"The Bronx Martini" illustration for a calendar featuring a different
drink for each month.
Watercolor and pen and ink.

202

Barbara Nessim Artist
Barbara Nessim and Mare Early Art Directors
Barbara Nessim and Mare Early Copywriters
Barbara Nessim Graphics Advertising Agency
Scarlett Letters Client

Poster with the copyline "A New Face Communicates"
to advertise new type faces.
Watercolor and pen and ink.

203

Barbara Nessim Artist
Henry Roth and Freddie White Art Directors
American Cancer Society Client

Poster with the copyline "Get in Touch with Your Body"
for doctors' offices, hospitals and clinics.
Pen and ink.

204

John Martinez Artist
John Martinez Art Director

Limited edition poster, September 1981.
Serigraphy from cut paper.

205

John Martinez Artist
John Martinez Art Director
Mirage Editions Client

Limited edition poster, April 1981.
Serigraphy from cut paper.

206

Doug Johnson Artist
Terry Watson Art Director
Gilmore Advertising Company Advertising Agency
Upjohn Client

Color poster to advertise "Pantherfoot"
chemical process for making running shoes.
Dyes and gouache.

207

Barbara Klunder Artist
Joanne Othuis Designer
Bob Russell Creative Director
Sharpshooter Productions Client

Self-promotion poster, November 1981.
Colored pencils.

208

Richard Mantel Artist
Sandra Ruch Art Director
Fran Michelman Copywriter
Mobil Corp. Client

Bus stop and subway poster to publicize a
Masterpiece Theater television program, "The Flame Trees of Thika,"
with the copyline "As a child she left the misty shores
of England for an Eden in Africa."
Acrylic.

209
Richard Mantel Artist
Richard Mantel Art Director
Tony Hitchcock Copywriter
The Hampton Classic Client

Illustration for a poster to advertise the Hampton Classic Annual
Horse Show in Bridgehampton, Long Island, August 1981.
Acrylic.

210

Jose Cruz Artist
Brian Boyd Art Director
Larry Sons Copywriter
Richard, Sullivan & Brock Advertising Agency
Harper House Client

Poster used for promotional mailing to
illustrate four-color process painting.
Acrylic.

211

Michael Schwab Artist
Michael Schwab Design Design Group

"The Swimmer" self-promotion poster.
Eight-color lithograph.

212
Milton Glaser Artist
Milton Glaser Art Director
Milton Glaser, Inc. Advertising Agency
The Overlook Press Client

Color poster to advertise the tenth anniversary
of The Overlook Press.
Colored ink.

213

Milton Glaser Artist
Milton Glaser Art Director
Milton Glaser, Inc. Advertising Agency
Saratoga Performing Arts Center Client

Poster to advertise Saratoga Performing Arts Center,
with the copyline S.P.A.C., July 1981.
Colored ink.

214

Milton Glaser Artist
Milton Glaser Art Director
Milton Glaser, Inc. Advertising Agency
San Francisco Opera Client

Poster for outdoor ad and for magazines to publicize San Francisco
Opera Summer Festival Concerts, April 1981.
Colored ink.

215

Gary Panter Artist
Gary Panter Art Director
Pee Wee Herman Productions Client

Poster to advertise The
Pee Wee Herman Show, January 1981.
Ink and cut paper.

Jeff Jackson Artist
David Menear Designer
Stewart Hood Art Director
Rob Ramsay and Doug Knight Copywriters
Financial Post Publication
The Jerry Goodis Agency, Inc. Advertising Agency

Poster used to advertise Financial Post newspaper
with the copyline, "Financial Most."
Colored pencil on tracing paper.

217

Teresa Fasolino Artist
Milton Glaser Art Director
Julia Koenig Copywriter
Milton Glaser Inc. Advertising Agency
Grand Union Client

"Poultry in Landscape" poster with the slogan "Grand Union's Fine
Fowl" appearing in Grand Union supermarkets.
Acrylic.

218

Bill Nelson Artist
Bill Nelson Art Director
Mobility Inc. Client

"The Actor" limited edition print, used as self-promotion
for both artist and printing company.
Colored pencil and watercolor.

219

Bill Nelson Artist
Bill Nelson Art Director
Bill Nelson Copywriter
The Poster Gallery Client

Poster to promote a one-man show.
Colored pencil.

Promotion

This section includes work commissioned for calendars, diaries, direct mail announcements, greeting cards, packaging, promotional brochures, promotional mailings, record sleeves, stationery, technical and industrial catalogs.

TWO FULL-LENGTH VERSIONS NEWLY REMASTERED IN SPECTACULAR SOUND!

B O L E R O
RAVEL

LEONARD BERNSTEIN
ORCHESTRE NATIONAL DE FRANCE

MX 35860

MASTER WORKS CBS

PLUS B O L E R O O N T H E M I G H T Y M O O G
A VIRTUOSO SYNTHESIZER PERFORMANCE BY ANDREW KAZDIN AND THOMAS Z. SHEPARD

222
David Wilcox Artist
Henrietta Condak Designer
Henrietta Condak Art Director
CBS Records Client

Record sleeve illustration for the album "Ravel's Bolero,"
conducted by Leonard Bernstein, 1980.
Acrylic.

223
David Wilcox Artist
Paula Scher and Gene Grief Designers
Paula Scher Art Director
CBS Records Client

Record sleeve design for "Shine the Light of Love,"
featuring Googie and Tom Coppola, 1981.
Acrylic.

Text on ticket:

CARNEGIE HALL
DOROTHY CHANDLER PAVILION

**ONE-NIGHT STAND
A KEYBOARD EVENT**

Kenny Barron, Eubie Blake, Arthur Blythe, Stanley Clarke, George Duke,
Charles Earland, Rodney Franklin, Herbie Hancock, Sir Roland Hanna,
Bobby Hutcherson, Bob James, Hubert Laws, Ramsey Lewis, Buddy Williams

David Wilcox Artist
Allen Weinberg Designer
Allen Weinberg Art Director
CBS Records Client

Record sleeve design for "One-Night Stand—A Keyboard Event,"
featuring various artists, 1981.
Acrylic.

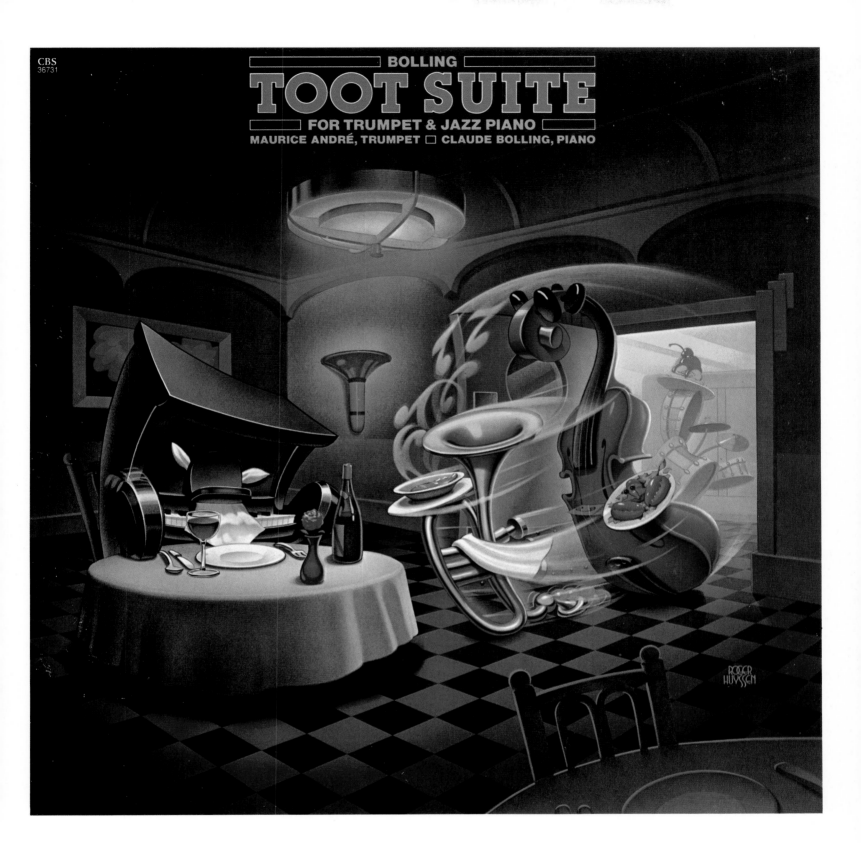

225

Roger Huyssen Artist
John Berg Designer
John Berg Art Director
CBS Records Client

Record sleeve design for "Toot Suite," an album featuring
Michel Andre, trumpet, and Claude Bolling, piano, 1981.
Gouache and anolin dye.

226

William Sloan Artist

Self-promotion piece entitled "They've Taken the Moon Away."
Part of the artist's portfolio.
Colored pencil and ink.

227

Katheryn Holt Artist
Katherine Holt Designer
Katheryn Holt Art Director
Paper Moon Graphics Publisher

Drawing for a greeting card
commissioned by Paper Moon Graphics, 1981.
Prisma color, airbrush.

Jaromir Weinberger
First Recording / Premier Enregistrement / Schallplattenpremiere
79344
36926
SCHWANDA
The Bagpiper / Der Dudelsackpfeifer / Le Joueur de cornemuse
MASTER CBS WORKS
Lucia
Popp
Siegfried
Jerusalem
Hermann
Prey
Gwendolyn
Killebrew
Siegmund
Nimsgern
Heinz
Wallberg
Munich Radio Orchestra / Münchener Rundfunk Orchester

228

Dagmar Frinta Artist
Christopher Austopchuk Art Director
Christopher Austopchuk Designer
CBS Records Client

Record sleeve illustration for "Schwanda the Bagpiper," an album featuring the Munich Radio Orchestra, 1982.
Acrylic.

Endless Beach

229

Elwood H. Smith Artist
Paula Scher Designer
Paula Scher Art Director
CBS Records Client

Record sleeve illustration for "Endless Beach,"
an album featuring various artists, 1982.
Watercolor.

230

Terry Widener Artist
Terry Widener Art Director

"Diner" self-promotion piece. Part of the artist's portfolio,
January 1982.
Gouache.

231

Jane Kleinman Artist
Jane Kleinman Designer
William Baron Art Director
Cartier Inc. Client

"The Cartier Woman" illustration used for
display in Cartier jewelry store.
Pastel, spray paint and make-up.

232

Terry Allen Artist
Terry Allen Designer
Jim Richards Art Director
Compugraphic Client
Media Concepts Advertising Agency

Illustration entitled "Fits Like a Glove" used as a brochure
to promote new computer typesetter.
Pen and ink with airbrush.

233

Lili Lakich Artist
Lili Lakich Designer
Lili Lakich Art Director
Scott & Daughter Publishing Publisher

"Mona," divider page for makeup section
in California Workbook and also used as corporate image
for Museum of Neon Art, September 1981.
Neon and photostat.

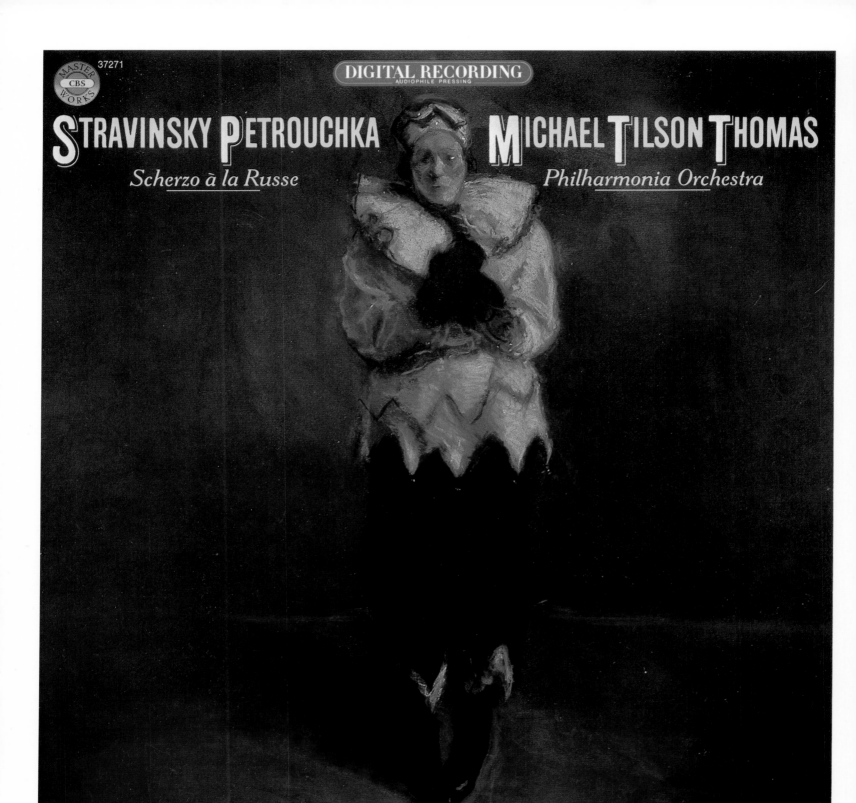

STRAVINSKY PETROUCHKA MICHAEL TILSON THOMAS
Scherzo à la Russe *Philharmonia Orchestra*

DIGITAL RECORDING
AUDIOPHILE PRESSING

MASTER WORKS CBS

37271

234

John Collier Artist
Henrietta Condak Art Director
CBS Records Client

Record sleeve design for "Stravinsky Petrouchka," an album featuring
Michael Tilson Thomas Philharmonia Orchestra, 1982.
Pastel.

235

Jerry McDonald Artist
Tony Lane Designer
Tony Lane Art Director
CBS Records Client

Design for the record album "Magic Moment,"
featuring Marcio Montarroyos, 1982.
Pen and ink, airbrush and Dr. Martin dyes.

236

Jose Cruz Artist
Matt Watson and Jose Cruz Designers
Matt Watson and Jose Cruz Art Directors
Thompson Press Publisher
Matt Watson Design Design Group

Illustration of Japanese fish for datebook published January 1982.
Acrylic.

237

Nick Taggart Artist

Advertisement in Stuff Magazine to
publicize the artist's work, June 1981.
Acrylic.

238

James C. Christensen Artist
James C. Christensen Designer
Michael Graves Art Director
Springville Museum of Art Client

"Card Game at Latours" illustration used as self-promotion brochure
for one-man show at Springville Museum of Art.
Acrylic.

239
David Montiel Artist
David Montiel Designer
David Montiel Art Director

"Mangos de Mexico" self-promotion illustration used as a promotional
mailer/card. Part of the artist's portfolio.
Acrylic on canvas.

240

Milton Glaser Artist
Milton Glaser Designer
Milton Glaser Art Director
Robert Palmer Writer
Atlantic Deluxe/The Atlantic Record Co. Client

Record sleeve illustration for the album
"Albert King Masterworks," April 1982.
Colored pencil and crayon and brown ink.

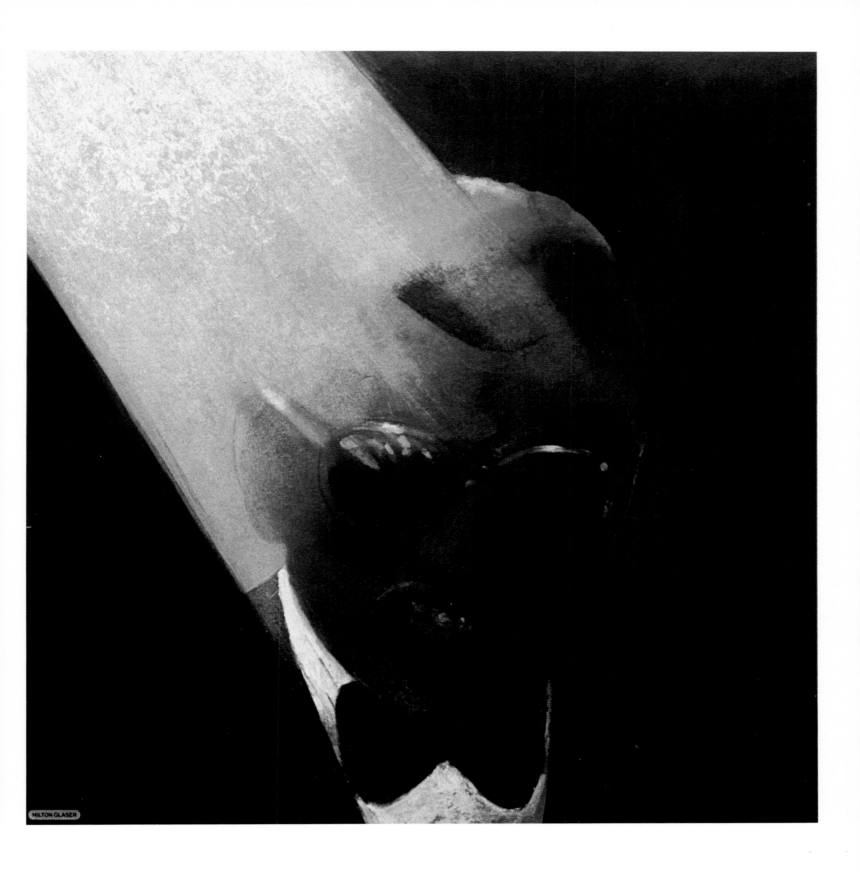

241

Milton Glaser Artist
Milton Glaser Designer
Milton Glaser Art Director
Nat Hentoff Writer
Atlantic Deluxe/The Atlantic Record Co. Client

Record sleeve illustration for "A Life in the Music,"
featuring Ray Charles, April 1982.
Pen and ink, colored ink and crayon.

242

Edward Sorel Artist
Edward Sorel Designer
Backstroms Repro Publisher

"Wedded Bliss," one of a series of drawings
for the publisher, January 1981.
Pen and ink and watercolor.

Unpublished

This section includes commissioned
but unpublished illustrations,
personal work produced by professionals,
and the work of students.

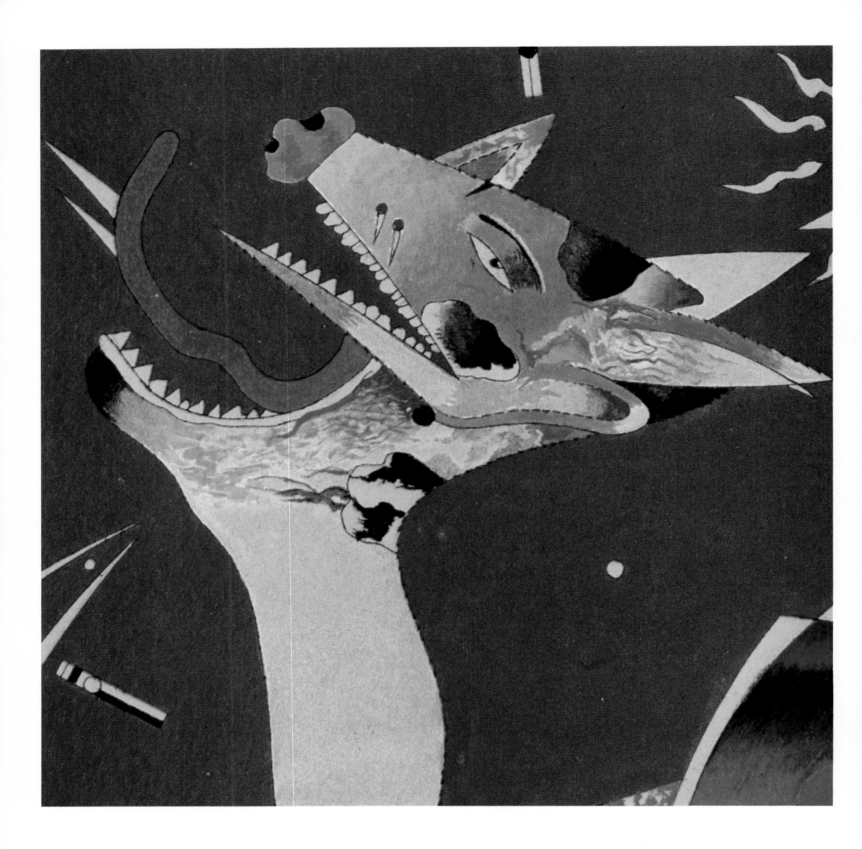

244

Sue Llewellyn Artist

"Dog Force," unpublished personal work by artist.
Acrylic.

245

Vivienne Flesher Artist
Ron Kellum Art Director

Commissioned but unused portrait for RCA
record album cover entitled "Piatogorsky," 1981.
Watercolor and pastel.

246

Kim Carlson Artist

Drawing to depict silent comic
film star Harold Lloyd.
Acrylic.

247

Mary Yanish Artist

Portrait.
Acrylic on canvas.

248

Bart Goldman Artist

Untitled work for the artist's portfolio.
Acrylic and alkyd.

249
Karen McDonald Artist

Untitled work for artist's portfolio.
Pastel.

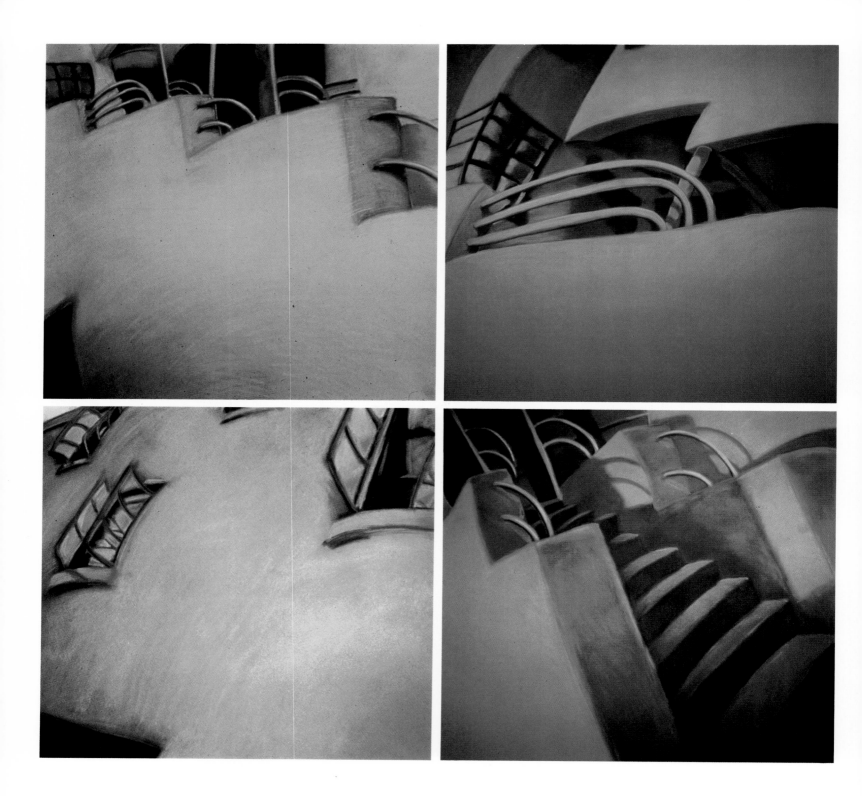

250, 251

Karen McDonald Artist

Unpublished series of five illustrations.
Pastel.

Karen McDonald Artist

Untitled work for artist's portfolio.
Pastel.

253

Karen McDonald Artist

Untitled work for artist's portfolio.
Pastel.

254

Marvin Mattelson Artist

Cover illustration commissioned, but unpublished, by Time
magazine for a feature entitled "Louise Nevelson."
Acrylic.

255

Meredith Nemirov Artist

"Triple Self-Portrait," part of the artist's portfolio.
Watercolor and gouache.

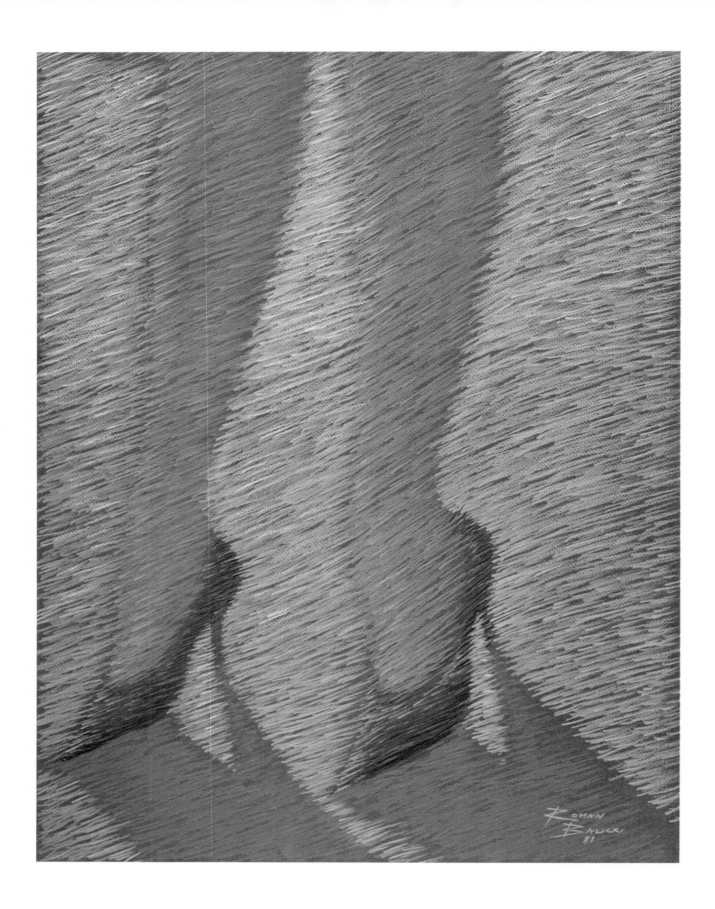

256

Roman Balicki Artist

Drawing entitled "Stiletto."
Part of the artist's portfolio.
Colored pencil.

257

Roman Balicki Artist

Drawing entitled "On the Beach."
Part of the artist's portfolio.
Black ink and airbrush.

Judy Pedersen Artist
Drawing for the artist's portfolio.
Pastel.

259

Martin Sigmund Artist

Personal work by artist entitled "Nostalgic Fantasy."
Acrylic.

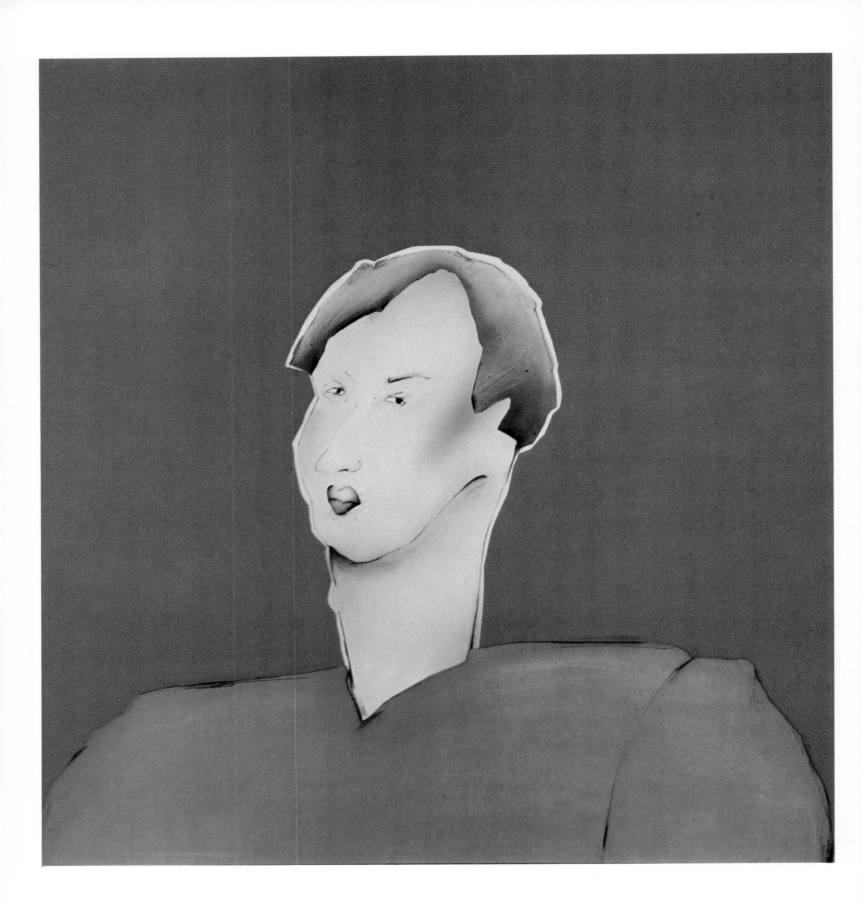

260
Gary Mele Artist

Untitled portrait, part of the artist's portfolio.
Mixed media.

261

Vivienne Flesher Artist

Self-promotion piece. Part of the artist's portfolio.
Oil paint and pastel.

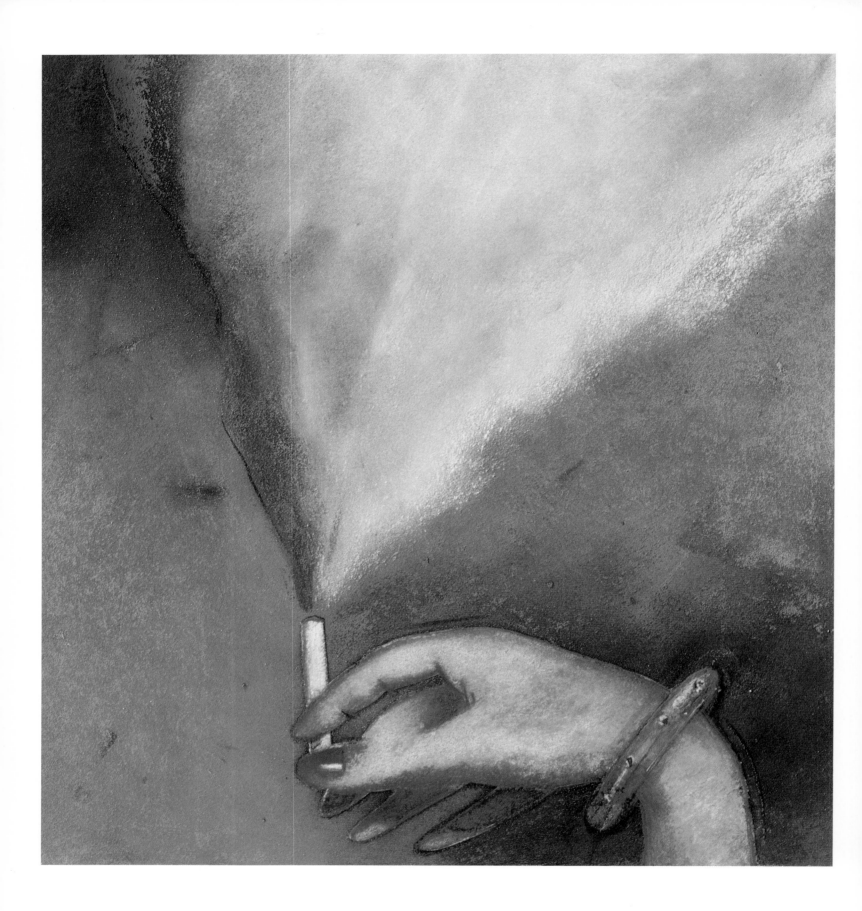

262

Vivienne Flesher Artist

Self-promotion piece. Part of the artist's portfolio.
Pastels.

263

Vivienne Flesher Artist

Untitled drawing used for self-promotion.
Part of the artist's portfolio.
Pastels and watercolor.

Vivienne Flesher Artist

Untitled drawing. Part of the artist's portfolio.
Oil paint and pastel.

265

Vivienne Flesher Artist

Self-promotion piece,
part of the artist's portfolio.
Pastel and watercolor.

266

Mike Quon Artist

"Chinese Zodiac," one of a series of illustrations for posters.
Unpublished.
Ink and plastic adhesives.

267

Barbara Nessim Artist
Barbara Nessim Art Director
Barbara Nessim Designer
Barbara Nessim Author

Book illustration for 'Stories Mother Never Told Me'.
Unpublished personal work.
Gouache.

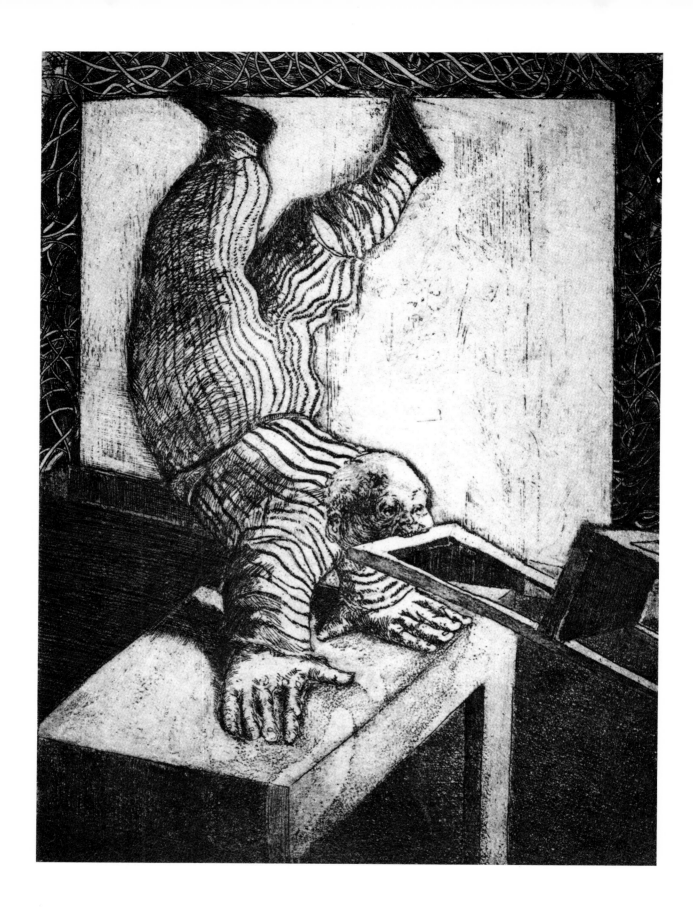

268

Kathryn Jacobi Artist

"The Acrobat," one of a series of 40 etchings illustrating
'Invitation to a Beheading' by Vladimir Nabokov. Personal work by
the artist.
Intaglio.

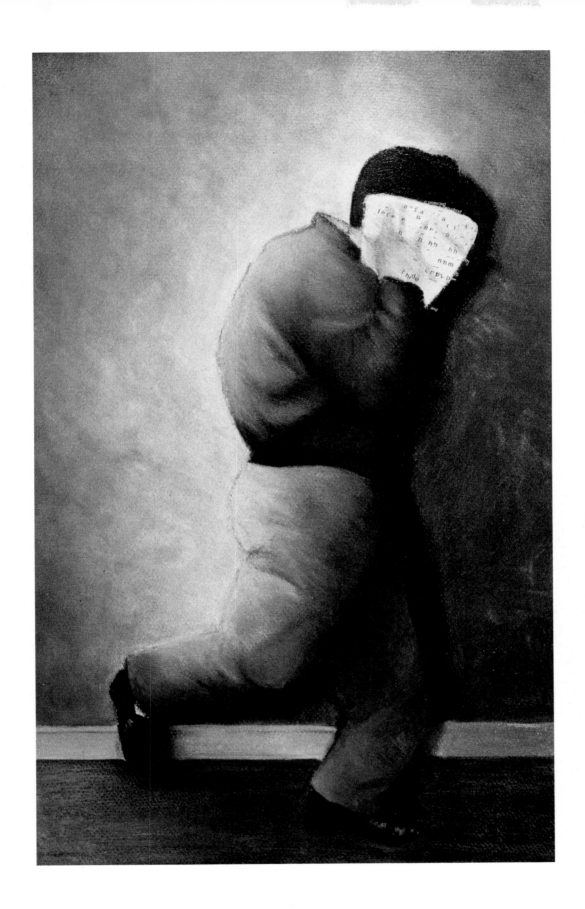

269

Sandra Dionisi Artist

"Misled Youth," illustration that deals with the subject of teenage
delinquency. Part of the artist's portfolio as a student at the
Ontario College of Art.
Oil, pastels and turpentine.

270

Alexa Grace Artist

Unpublished boxed sculpture drawing for a show at the Graham
Gallery entitled "You May Be Luckier Than You Think."
Porcelain, sandpaper and paint.

271

Alexa Grace Artist
Christopher Austopchuk Art Director

Unpublished work commissioned by CBS Records for the album
"Death and the Maiden," featuring the Julliard Quartet.
Three-dimensional relief on tarpaper.

272

Cathryn Schwing Artist

"Tea Eggs," one of a series of illustrations for an egg cookbook. Part of
the artist's
portfolio used for self-promotion.
Colored pencil and serigraphy.

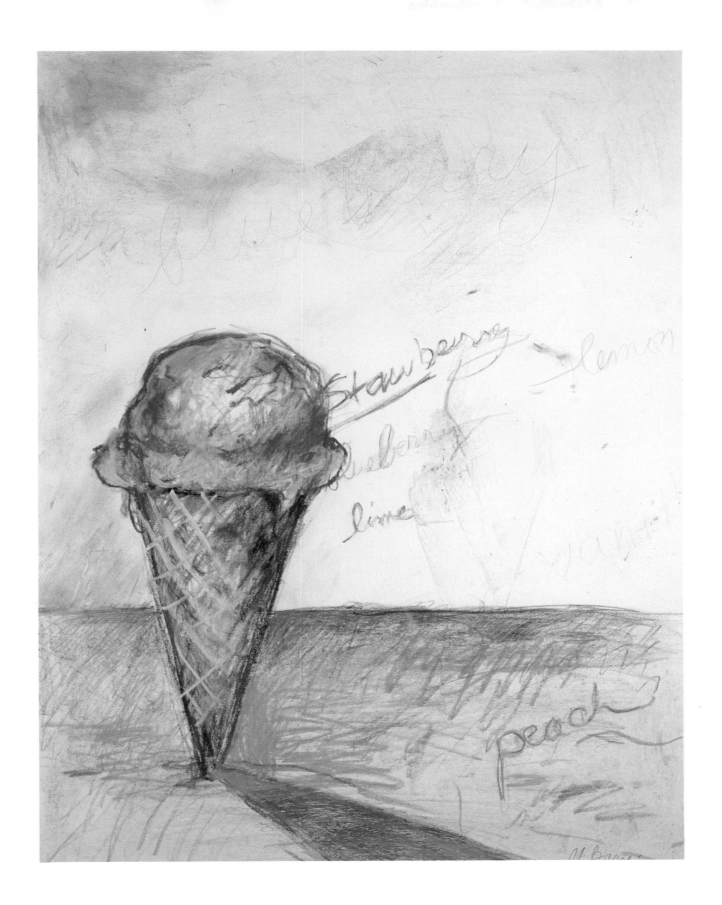

273

Michelle Barnes Artist

One of a series of ten illustrations commissioned,
but not used, by Harrigon's Ice Cream Shop.
Crayon and pastel.

274

Scott Reynolds Artist

Unpublished portrait of Billie Holliday.
Pastel, oil paint and spray paint.

275

Scott Reynolds Artist

Unpublished illustration of a 1956 Oldsmobile
flashing through the night.
Pastel.

276

Scott Reynolds Artist

Unpublished portrait of
two classical cigarette packages.
Xerox on acetate with pastel and oil.

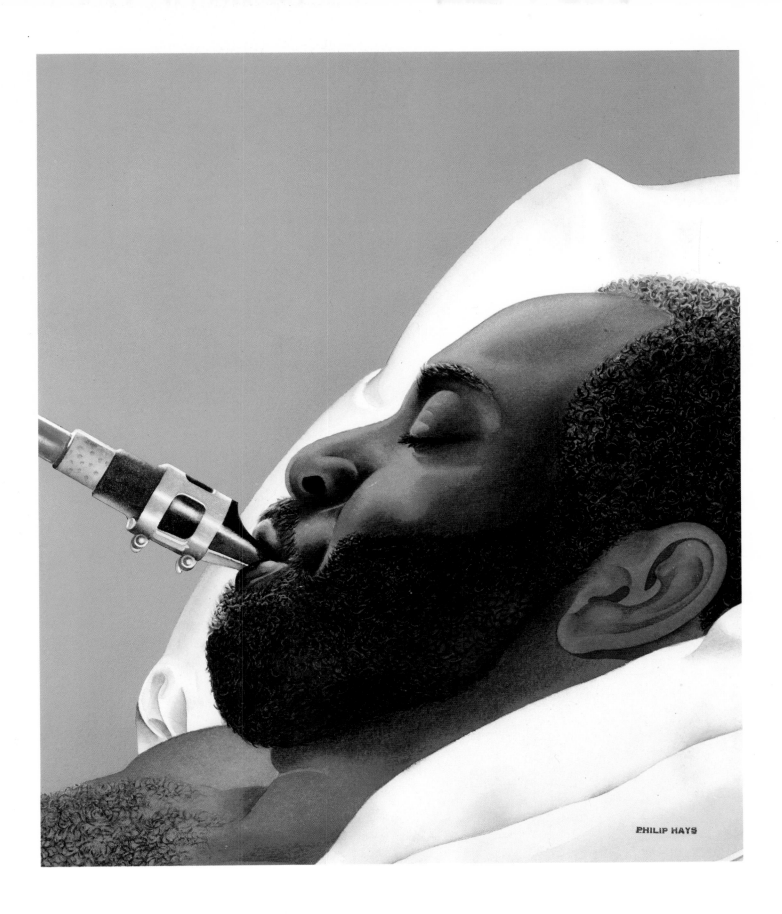

277

Philip Hays Artist

Illustration for a record sleeve commissioned,
but unpublished, by Motown Records for an album
featuring Grover Washington, Jr.
Watercolor.

278

Amie Weitzman Artist

Illustration for an article entitled "Single Woman in the City."
Done while artist was studing at Parsons School of Design.
Gouache.

279

Patric FoURshé Artist

Illustration to depict the comforts of home.
Casein and acrylic.

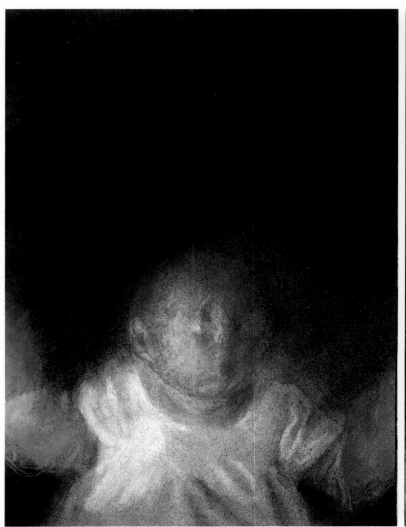 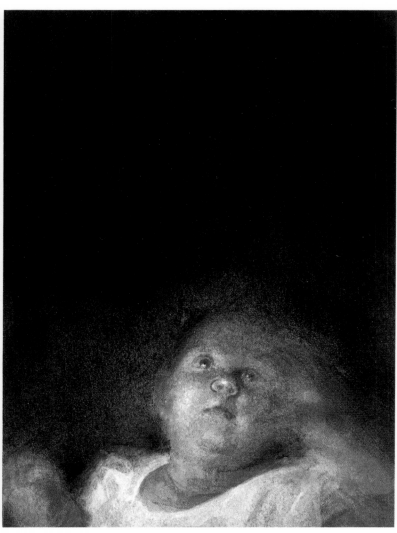

280

Thomas Woodruff Artist

"Bust," two images from a series of
fifteen paintings with text. Personal work.
Watercolor, powdered charcoal and acrylic.

Film

This section includes film animation for
television, advertising and short films.

282

Tissa David Animator
R.O. Blechman Artist
R.O. Blechman Director
Marty Kaufman Writer
Hy Varon Art Director
Lois Goldberg and Herb Miller Agency Producers
Arnold Black Music Composer
Leber Katz Partners Agency
Ink Tank Production Company
IBM Client

Commercial animated film to publicize
IBM Datamaster entitled "Freedom."

Tissa David and Tony Eastman Animators
Seymour Chwast Artist
R.O. Blechman Director
Cliff Freeman Writer
Jean Govoni Art Director
Janet Fogarty Producer
Arnold Black Music Composer
Dancer Fitzgerald Sample, Inc. Agency
Ink Tank Production Company
General Mills Client

A commercial animated film to publicize
Yoplait yogurt entitled "Dick Tracy."

Dale Case, Pam Cooke, Alan Zaslove Animators
Robert Peluce Artist
Bob Kurtz Director
Reyn Bowman Producer
Kurtz & Friends Production Company
Anchorage Convention Bureau Client

Commercial animated film entitled "Wild About Anchorage" to
advertise Anchorage Convention Bureau.

Index

Names and addresses of contributing artists. Index of designers, art directors, art editors, publications, publishers, design groups, advertising agencies, copywriters, editors, animators, film directors, producers, production companies and clients.

Judy Pedersen 258
96 Greene Street
New York, New York
10012

Robert Peluce 284
c/o Kurtz & Friends
1728 N. Whitley Avenue
Hollywood, California
90028

Paola Piglia 128, 141
100 West 87th Street
#3A
New York, New York
10024

Ian Pollock 145
Flat 6
21 Pleshey Road
London N70RA
England

Don Ivan Punchatz 27
Sketchpad Studio
2605 Westgate Drive
Arlington, Texas 76015

Liz Pyle 53, 75, 108, 109,
113
6 Barnsbury Square
London N1 England

Mike Quon 266
53 Spring Street
New York, New York
10012

Joel Resnicoff 124
c/o Carolyn Brindle
203 East 89th Street
New York, New York
10028

Scott Reynolds 137, 274,
275, 276
308 West 30th Street
#9B
New York, New York
10001

Michael Schwab 211
410 Townsend
San Francisco,
California 94107

Cathryn Schwing 272
1006 Palisade Avenue
#14
Union City, New Jersey
07087

Martin Sigmund 259
Double Vision
167 East 73rd Street
New York, New York
10021

William A. Sloan 226
444 East 82nd Street
#12C
New York, New York
10028

Doug Smith 99
405 Washington
Brookline,
Massachusetts
02146

Elwood H. Smith 73, 96,
229
Pushpin Lubalin
Peckolick, Inc.
67 Irving Place
New York, New York
10003

Jeffrey J. Smith 100
317 E. Sidney Avenue
Mt. Vernon, New York
10553

Edward Sorel 51, 199, 242
156 Franklin Street
New York, New York
10013

Ralph Steadman 94, 95
c/o Nat Sobel
128 East 56th Street
New York, New York
10022

Dugald Stermer 177
1844 Union Street
San Francisco,
California 94123

David Suter 84
31 Union Square
New York, New York
10003

Nick Taggart 237
2643 Crestmore
Los Angeles, California
90065

Cristobal Toral 52
c/o Russ Melcher
38 Allee St. Andrew
Domain de la Tuilerie
78590 Noisy Le Roi
France

James Tughan 144
87 Mowatt Avenue #204
Toronto, Ontario
M6K3E3
Canada

Michel Guiré Vaka 21
74 rue Hallé
Paris 14e France 75014

Karen Watson 62
6A Walnut Avenue
Cambridge
Massachusetts 02140

Amie Weitzman 278
42 West 13th Street #5A
New York, New York
10011

Terry Widener 230
10161 Casa View
Dallas, Texas 75228

David Wilcox 104, 186,
222, 223, 224
P.O. Box 232
So. Main Street
Califon, New Jersey
07830

Thomas Woodruff 29,
153, 280
29 Cornelia Street
New York, New York
10014

Janet Woolley 35, 70, 105
34 Stanhope Road
Highgate, London
N65NG
England

Mary Yanish 247
3887 Bostwick Street
Los Angeles, California
90063

Dennis Ziemienski 134
121 West 3rd Street
New York, New York
10012

DESIGNERS

Catherine Aldrich 99,
157, 159
Terry Allen 232
Christopher
Austopchuk 228
Roman Balicki 146
Carl Barile 180, 181
Bascove 170
John Berg 225
R.O. Blechman 47
Richard Boddy 65
Caroline Bowyer 108,
109, 138, 139
Braldt Bralds 154
Joe Brooks 19
Philip Burke 110
Ronn Campisi 33, 62, 63,
68, 86, 111, 115, 131, 157,
158
Patricia Candor 171
Steve Carver 71
James C. Christensen
238
Henrietta Condak 222
Stephen Costello 34, 143
Jose Cruz 236
Andrea Da Rif 119
Frank Devino 20
Stephen Doyle 105
Louise Fili 168, 169, 175,
176, 178
Louis Fishauf 17
B.J. Galbraith 72
Judy Garlan 51, 126, 127,
142, 150
Milton Glaser 240, 241
Martine Gourbault 22
Gene Grief 223
Bruce Hansen 48
Phil Hays 195
Steve Heller 98, 172, 173
Richard Hendel 166
Rudolph Hoglund 132
Nigel Holmes 84
Katheryn Holt 227
Jane Kleinman 231
Karen Klingon 128
Theo Kouvatsos 116
Jerelle Kraus 123
Stephen Kroninger 110
Diane Lamphron 40
Tony Lane 235
Lili Lakich 233
Sue Llewellyn 60
Richard Mantel 140, 151

James McMullan 90, 195
David Meanear 216
Sara Midda 163, 164, 165
David Montiel 239
Françoise Mouly 155
Barbara Nessim 267
Art Niemi 39, 120, 121
Mary Opper 82, 83, 85,
113, 148
Joanne Othuis 207
Greg Paul 130
Patty Pecoraro 179
B. Martin Pedersen 112,
152
Janet Perr 125
Kerig Pope 23, 45, 54,
58, 59, 129
Robert Post 64
Robert Priest 49
Franco Raggi 36
Bruce Ramsay 70, 77,
136, 149, 156
Joel Resnicoff 124
Nancy Rice 28, 46
Muney Rivers 21
Ellen Rongstad 69, 87,
135
Nina Scerbo 26
Paula Scher 223, 229
Tamara Schneider 117
April Silver 25, 29, 35,
42, 43, 53, 57, 73, 79, 97,
145, 153
Edward Sorel 242
Art Spiegelman 155
Lynn Staley 102, 103,
122
Dugald Stermer 177
James Tughan 144
Derek Ungless 76
Vincent Winter 24
Matt Watson 236
Claire Victor 41, 52, 61,
89, 94, 95, 104, 133
Allen Weinberg 224
Mary Zisk 30, 31

ART DIRECTORS

Miles Abernathy 66
Tina Adamek 28, 46
Dick Adleson 170
Christopher Austopchak
81, 228, 271
William Baron 231
Brad Benedict 167
Dianne Benson 185
John Berg 225
Caroline Bowyer 108,
109, 138, 139
Brian Boyd 210
Michael Brock 154
Joe Brooks 19, 27, 41, 52,
61, 89, 94, 95, 104, 133
Philip Burke 110
Ronn Campisi 33, 62, 63,
68, 86, 99, 111, 115, 131,
147, 157, 158, 159
Patricia Candor 171
Seymour Chwast 140,
151, 187, 196, 198
Henrietta Condak 222,
234
Stephen Costello 34, 39,
120, 121, 143
Jose Cruz 236
Andrea Da Rif 119
Frank Devino 20
Stephen Doyle 105

Mare Early 202
Lidia Ferrara 162
Louise Fili 168, 169, 175,
176, 178
Louis Fishauf 17, 194
Bruce Fitzgerald 124
Barbara Francis 180, 181
B.J. Galbraith 72
Judy Garlan 51, 78, 91,
92, 93, 126, 127, 142, 150
Pat Garling 137
Milton Glaser 212, 213,
214, 217, 240, 241
Martine Gourbault 22
Jean Govoni 283
Michael Graves 238
Gene Grief 67
George Grodzicki 184
Michael Grossman 44
Paul Hansen 163, 164,
165
Phil Hays 195
Steve Heller 98, 172, 173
Richard Hendel 166
Fred Hilliard 192
Rudolph Hoglund 84,
101, 132
Nigel Holmes 84
Katheryn Holt 227
Stewart Hood 216
James Ireland 88
Doug Johnson 200
Skip Johnston 18
Chris Jones 75
Ron Kellum 245
Bill Kobasz 96
Louise Kollenbaum 38
Terry Koppel 37
Jerelle Kraus 123
Stephen Kroninger 110
Diane Lamphron 40
Tony Lane 235
Lili Lakich 233
Anne Leigh 200
Richard Mantel 209
John Martinez 204, 205
Brad McIver 146
David Montiel 239
Francoise Mouly 155
Bill Nelson 218, 219
Barbara Nessim 202,
267
Susan Niles 128
Gary Panter 215
Russell Patrick 188, 189,
190
Greg Paul 32, 80, 106,
107, 130
Patty Pecoraro 179
B. Martin Pedersen 112,
152
Janet Perr 71, 125
Michael V. Phillips 186
Kerig Pope, 55
Robert Priest 21, 25, 29,
35, 42, 43, 49, 53, 57, 65,
69, 73, 79, 87, 97, 135,
141, 145, 153
Franco Raggi 36
Susan Reinhardt 47, 56
Jim Richards 232
Rosamaria Rinaldi 36
Ken Rodmell 114
Henry Roth 203
Sandra Ruch 208
Bob Russell 207
Nina Scerbo 26
Paula Scher 223, 229
Tamara Schneider 117

Cynthia Schupf 193
Howard Shintaku 134
April Silver 141
Barbara Solowan 88
Edward Sorel 199
Art Spiegelman 155
Tom Staebler 23, 45, 48,
54, 58, 59, 64, 116, 129
Lynn Staley 102, 103,
122
Dugald Stermer 177
Sherri Thompson 100
Shinichiro Tora 201
Derek Ungless 70, 76,
77, 82, 83, 85, 113, 136,
148, 149, 156
Hy Varon 282
Matt Watson 236
Terry Watson 206
Allen Weinberg 224
Freddie White 203
Terry Widener 230
Vincent Winter 24
Fred Woodward 60
Jackie Young 144
Mary Zisk 30, 31

PUBLISHERS

A & W Publishers, Inc.
172, 173
Active Markets, Inc. 24
Alfred A. Knopf, Inc. 162
Art Center College of
Design 195
Atlantic Monthly Co. 51,
78, 91, 92, 93, 126, 127,
142, 150
Backstroms Repro 242
Comac Communications
Ltd. 34, 39, 120, 121, 143
Condé Nast
Publications, Inc. 128
Cycle Guide
Publications, Inc. 137
Dell Publishing Co., Inc.
179
Dow Jones & Co. 108,
109, 138, 139
Esquire Publishing, Inc.
21, 25, 29, 35, 42, 43, 49,
53, 57, 65, 69, 73, 79, 87,
97, 135, 141, 145, 153
Fouundation for
National Progress 38
Globe Newspaper
Company 33, 37, 62, 63,
68, 86, 99, 102, 103, 111,
115, 122, 131, 147, 157,
158, 159
Graphis Press Corp. 90
Harmony Books 167
The Hearst Corp. 30, 31,
160
Heather & Pine
International, Inc. 119
IPC Magazines Ltd. 75
Key Publishers 88, 114,
146
Lancaster-Miller
Publishers 177
Laurant Publishing Ltd.
154
McCall Publishing Co.
26
McGraw-Hill, Inc. 28, 46
Ms Magazine Corp. 40
Nautical Quarterly Co.
112, 152

289

AMERICAN ILLUSTRATION

American Illustration was created in June 1981 to
select, each year, a truly representative collection of
illustration in America, done not only by professionals
but by students as well.
Every year a jury, picked from across the country,
will meet in March and choose work for the yearly
book and exhibition. To coincide with the publication,
a symposium on illustration will be held each year in
October.
The Committee's aim is:
A) To give recognition to high standards of
illustration and to encourage the development of up-
and-coming illustrators and artists who will lead the
way in bringing to the surface the many talents of the
different cultures that exist in America today, and
B) To promote North American illustrators
throughout the world through this Annual and by
exhibitions of original artwork. The first planned
show of art will be in Paris.

Executive Committee:
Julian Allen,
Illustrator
Marshall Arisman,
Illustrator and Co-Chairperson, Media Arts,
School of Visual Arts of New York
Ronn Campisi,
Chief Designer, Boston Globe
Rudy Hoglund,
Art Director, Time Magazine
Steve Heller,
Art Director, New York Times Book Review
Linda Johnson,
Freelance Art Director
John Macfarlane,
Publisher, Saturday Night Magazine, Toronto
Robert Priest,
Art Director, Esquire Magazine
Edward Booth-Clibborn,
Chairman
Lita Telerico,
Managing Editor

If you would like to
know more about the
activities of American
Illustration, and if you
are a practicing
illustrator, artist, or
student, and want to
submit work to the
annual competition,
write to:
Lita Telerico
American Illustration, Inc.
67 Irving Place
New York, NY 10003